"I believe *Translating Jesus* will help demystify and simplify conversations with culture about Christ. I equally believe these three sentences will be a fresh and winsome evangelistic tool and conversation guide: Jesus loves you. Love Him back. Love one another. Shauna has modeled this in wonderful ways. We'd do well to follow in her steps."

Rich Villodas, lead pastor of New Life Fellowship
and author of *The Deeply Formed Life*

"In an era when too many Christians are waging war on the culture or retreating from it, Shauna Pilgreen gives us a thoughtful, loving, practical advance."

Carey Nieuwhof, bestselling author of *At Your Best*
and founder of The Art of Leadership Academy

"Why would people believe that the God we are talking about wants to know them, if we don't want to know them? Could our open doors, ordinary tables, and honest conversations matter more than we know? In these practical yet stunningly personal pages, Shauna Pilgreen provides a hands-on guide for Christ-followers to graciously and effectively share about Jesus through their everyday conversations and their real relationships. *Translating Jesus* is a gift to today's local and global church—it's a love letter to Jesus and a guide to loving people well, written by someone who is clearly in close proximity to both."

Hosanna Wong, international speaker, spoken word artist,
and bestselling author of *How (Not) to Save the World*

"Shauna has written a beautiful and important book. The more post-Christian our society becomes, the more important it is to close the gap with though̶t̶ ̶ ̶ ̶ ̶ ̶b̶i̶b̶l̶i̶c̶a̶l̶ ̶m̶i̶s̶s̶i̶o̶n̶ and

T0049971

contextualization. Shauna has done a wonderful job on helping us think about how to love people to God and connect the gospel message in a timeless yet compelling way."

Pastor Jon Tyson, Church of the City New York, jon@church.nyc

"Shauna has an inspiring vision to share the love of God with those around her in a practical and accessible way. I am delighted she has written this book."

Nicky Gumbel, pioneer of Alpha

"For the last twelve years, I've watched Shauna live out the message of *Translating Jesus* in the beautiful, influential, and challenging city of San Francisco. It's been inspiring to see this Southern girl with four children embrace the city and the people of the city with such intentional love and curiosity. Shauna has put language to her learning in this book, and her personal stories will captivate you. Reading *Translating Jesus* helps me see how to invite Jesus into each interaction throughout everyday life. If every follower of Jesus embraced the principles of this book, it would change the world."

Stacie Wood, teaching pastor of Saddleback Church

"*Translating Jesus* is an urgent message for changing times. Shauna skillfully helps equip us from the inside out with the framework to deeply and lovingly engage with a fast-moving culture. The result is not just a new understanding of the power of the gospel but the ability to share the good news about Jesus with confidence. A must-read for anyone serious about communicating God's love to our generation."

Al Gordon, rector of SAINT, London

TRANSLATING
JESUS

Also by Shauna Pilgreen

Love Where You Live

TRANSLATING JESUS

HOW TO SHARE YOUR FAITH IN LANGUAGE

TODAY'S CULTURE CAN UNDERSTAND

SHAUNA PILGREEN

Revell

a division of Baker Publishing Group
Grand Rapids, Michigan

© 2023 by Shauna Pilgreen

Published by Revell
a division of Baker Publishing Group
Grand Rapids, Michigan
www.revellbooks.com

Printed in the United States of America

All rights reserved. No part of this publication may be reproduced, stored in a retrieval system, or transmitted in any form or by any means—for example, electronic, photocopy, recording—without the prior written permission of the publisher. The only exception is brief quotations in printed reviews.

Library of Congress Cataloging-in-Publication Data
Names: Pilgreen, Shauna, 1977– author.
Title: Translating Jesus : how to share your faith in language today's culture can understand / Shauna Pilgreen.
Description: Grand Rapids, Michigan : Revell, a division of Baker Publishing Group, [2023] | Includes bibliographical references.
Identifiers: LCCN 2022052002 | ISBN 9780800742508 (paperback)| ISBN 9780800744656 (casebound) | ISBN 9781493441402 (ebook)
Subjects: LCSH: Evangelistic work. | Communication—Religious aspects—Christianity. | Theology, Practical.
Classification: LCC BV3790 .P536 2023 | DDC 269/.2—dc23/eng/20230331
LC record available at https://lccn.loc.gov/2022052002

Unless otherwise indicated, Scripture quotations are from The Holy Bible, English Standard Version® (ESV®), copyright © 2001 by Crossway, a publishing ministry of Good News Publishers. Used by permission. All rights reserved. ESV Text Edition: 2016

Scripture quotations labeled CEB are from the Common English Bible. © Copyright 2011 by the Common English Bible. All rights reserved. Used by permission.

Scripture quotations labeled CEV are from the Contemporary English Version © 1991, 1992, 1995 by American Bible Society. Used by permission.

Scripture quotations labeled Message are from *THE MESSAGE*, copyright © 1993, 2002, 2018 by Eugene H. Peterson. Used by permission of NavPress. All rights reserved. Represented by Tyndale House Publishers, Inc.

Scripture quotations labeled NIV are from THE HOLY BIBLE, NEW INTERNATIONAL VERSION®, NIV® Copyright © 1973, 1978, 1984, 2011 by Biblica, Inc.® Used by permission. All rights reserved worldwide.

Scripture quotations labeled NLT are from the Holy Bible, New Living Translation, copyright © 1996, 2004, 2015 by Tyndale House Foundation. Used by permission of Tyndale House Publishers, Inc., Carol Stream, Illinois 60188. All rights reserved.

Scripture quotations labeled WEB are from the World English Bible.

The author is represented by The FEDD Agency, Inc.

Some names and details have been changed to protect the privacy of the individuals involved.

Baker Publishing Group publications use paper produced from sustainable forestry practices and post-consumer waste whenever possible.

23   24   25   26   27   28   29   7   6   5   4   3   2   1

To Epic Church, San Francisco,
and to Alpha friends worldwide

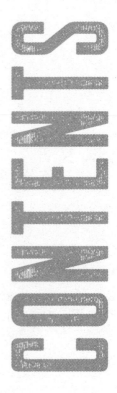

CONTENTS

Foreword

Shauna Pilgreen is one of my favorite writers. She's real. She's raw. And her books give me cause for pause. Not only is Shauna a wordsmith, she's a practitioner. She and her husband, Ben, lead an amazing church in San Francisco called Epic. That's how we first met. Ministry in the urban context is no joke! As someone who has pastored a church in the nation's capital for more than a quarter century, I have the utmost respect for leaders who play the long game. Ben and Shauna have done just that. They don't just talk the talk, they walk the walk.

In the pages that follow, you'll find real stories about real people. More than that, a real God with real solutions! Shauna's love for Jesus and His church bleeds through the pages. She's honest about the challenges we face. But this book is filled with hope. She takes us to the gate—the place where church and community cross paths. She takes us on a pilgrimage back to the foot of the cross, where the ground is level. And she saves a seat at the table, the place where Jesus did so much of His ministry.

You'll find one-liners you need to underline: "The language of Christ is prayer," or "Strangers aren't that strange," or "Sundays are for swapping stories." Don't read right over those insights. Let them seep into your soul. Shauna also introduces spiritual practices, like double listening, that will prove to be game changers if you put them into practice. This book is a page-turner, but I would warn against reading too fast.

One last recommendation? Find a comfortable chair and pour yourself a cup of coffee. This book is like hanging out with Shauna at your favorite coffee shop. Her authenticity and vulnerability are disarming, just like Jesus.

Mark Batterson, *New York Times* bestselling author of *The Circle Maker* and lead pastor at National Community Church

Introduction

I'm not great at sharing my faith. Sharing other things? No problem. What I like to do on vacation. Our favorite restaurants in
the city. The final play of the nail-biting game. The latest news
circling the globe. Those I can talk about because others are
interested, they care about the same things, or it affects their
lives. But my faith? I hesitate as if my faith encroaches on their
space, questions their beliefs, and makes conversations awkward. Who wants that?

But what if our faith in Jesus is what others are looking for?

I believe Jesus is real, and He loves every person around me.
I've experimented and concluded that if Christ followers pay
attention, we can speak to others about our faith.

We are communicating more than any generation before us,
but is anyone listening? We are trying to be understood, but the
people we talk to don't know our language. And what happens
when someone does not understand what we are saying? We talk
louder, as if that helps. Or we retreat to our own kind in hopes
they will validate our values. We spend time-consuming hours

with people who believe what we believe, and therefore we think we're living rightly. This keeps us polarized, which is exactly the plan—but not God's plan. The devil likes sides and likes when we only see two colors, black and white. It's never been more apparent that we desperately need to be able to understand one another.

Yet our faith in Jesus needs to be explained. *You mean you believe this guy is still alive? He did what? When was this? Yeah. No.* Our belief doesn't make sense to the outside world. This is what I seek to help you with.

I define *Christianity* as practicing the teachings of Jesus. I define a *Christian* as those who take the gospel, the Good News, to people who do not know and have not heard, which is what those folks in Acts 11:26 were up to. Christians are those who live up to the intended name of "little Christs," and I believe we can be respected by culture even if culture does not agree with us. I define *culture* as our part of the world and how it functions; the slice of the world we live in.

Oxford professor and theologian Alister McGrath wrote,

> Christianity needs to be explained. The Bible needs to be interpreted and applied. And both involve us, as active agents, doing our best to translate the realities of the gospel into the categories of the contemporary—not to reduce the gospel to contemporary ideas but to allow it to gain access to people's minds and lives, so that it can begin its work of transformation and renewal.[1]

I have non-Christian friends I do life with. I know their names, and they eat at our table and come to our church. We meet for coffee, sit beside each other in the baseball stands, give each other rides, and visit each other in the hospital. We get each other's mail, take each other food, and keep watch of each other's kids around town. You don't have to know non-Christians to read this book, but you can't live this book without having any as your friends.

Maybe you're frustrated with culture. Your heart has become callous toward people who just don't get it. Why bother trying to understand where they are coming from? Why take the time to listen to their different point of view? Why try to figure out your local context? **Because while you and I had our backs to God, He came near to us** (Rom. 5:8). He knocked on the door of your heart just like He is still knocking on other heart doors in this non-believing world. Jesus still finds them worth it. Do you? Now is not the time to turn your back on others. There are things we cannot do for anyone, but I've read my Bible; there are things we *can* do. We can invite God's presence into darkness. We can speak with courage and gentleness. Your non-believing friend might seem like the least likely person to come to Christ, but don't let that hold you back. Love them as Christ has loved you. Lay down your life—starting with your awkwardness, your discomfort—for your friends. This is how you translate Jesus.

So let me ask you, Are you burdened for your non-believing friends?

- Do you leave Christian gatherings excited about your faith, only to enter cultural contexts timid about your faith?
- Do you see things or have conversations where you wish you had the clarity and courage to bring up Jesus and how He's changing your life?

- Does your heart break over the unnecessary evils happening around you?
- Have you ever wanted to share your Jesus story?

If you answered yes to even one of these, you're in the right place, and you're going to learn a new way to share Jesus. Christianity is best explained when it's lived out. We, as we live, are the best way to translate Jesus. If you want people to know Jesus, be open for them to know you. We'll start by practicing two languages: Christ and culture.

Learn two languages.

You've been in these conversations before. Someone doesn't feel confident in their second language and continues to ask you to forgive them for having to stumble through their broken words to understand them. From your point of view, they're doing great, all things considered. This person, in the process of becoming bilingual, is a great model for us that it is better to practice than to shy away and neglect trying. This is how Christ taught us—speaking to His culture in ways they could relate to yet speaking the truth in love. As disciples of Jesus, we are to become bilingual.

These are learned languages. The language of Christ is *prayer*. In this book I'll talk about how to speak to Him, speak on behalf of others, pray on the spot, and teach this language to others. The language of culture is *attention*. This is the way every piece of society relates, sees the world, and talks with one another. It can be a spoken or unspoken language. Culture languages are generational and dialectic. Our teenagers have a way of speaking to their peers that we can't understand, and our teenagers don't always understand what their Southern grandmother is talking about! I'll help you learn how to pay attention, start conversations, tell your personal stories, and make friends with strangers.

Learning the language of Christ and culture to become bilingual mandates humility. This learning is fluid. It lacks walls and structure and echoes through one's being, boomeranging all over the senses, bringing kindness this world craves. Be open to discovery, to practice!

Be in three places.

We're going to three places where Christ spent time: the gate, the cross, and the table.

The gate represents today's communal spaces. It is everywhere we go when we are out and about. It's where we learn the language of culture. With our attentiveness and the Spirit's guidance, we are going to find companionship in unexpected places here.

The cross represents today's sacred spaces. When we are at the cross, we are at church, in Christian community, and having our personal time with Christ. It's where we engage in the language of Christ. We must come often and meet with other disciples. The life of a disciple is communal at its core. If we calculate the hours of His life on earth, Jesus spent the least amount of time at the cross, but our time at the gate and the table are powerless without the cross.

The table represents a collective of those we meet at the gate and the cross. We are in common places having intentional conversations with believers and non-believers. The table is where we become bilingual as we practice the language of Christ and the language of culture. We'll find ourselves having conversations where love leads and the Holy Spirit shows up.

The Jesus-disciple life is an active life. We'll begin to see one another and hear one another as we engage in all three places. It's also a back-and-forth life, and we'll live at all three places and pay attention to all three places. We were never intended to live only at one and not be attentive to the others. Together we will travel the two-way street between the gate, the cross, and the table, following Jesus into an overlapping, nonlinear life.

We don't just go from one stage to another in a single series of steps. While one of our friends is at the gate, another could be at the cross or the table. We meet them where they are. We might not be comfortable or fluent with the dominant language at that place, but we can be open-minded and openhanded at each stop.

You can become bilingual.

When I go to my favorite Italian restaurant in our city, I try out my best Italian while ordering. I always hesitate—a clear indicator to the server I'm a work in progress. As the choppy stutter comes out of my mouth, I am immediately hopeful the server can understand what dish I want and help me place my order. And he or she is always glad to help me and smiles because I'm trying. I've never gotten kicked out of the restaurant for practicing my Italian.

You speak a language at work. Whether it's coding or real estate or banking or medicine, there is a distinct language that helps those in your work culture understand one another.

When we sing at church about graves being turned into gardens, chains breaking, and no longer being slaves, we are using biblical language in a worship culture.

You follow Jesus, and He makes a lot of sense to you, but now that you have faith, it's as if you've forgotten how to talk! Who would understand you anyway? What you believe about Christ and your local context seem worlds apart.

As Alister McGrath wrote in *Mere Discipleship*, "Someone who is bilingual does not need a translator."[2] My hope and prayer as you read through this book is for Colossians 4:2–6 to come alive:

Continue steadfastly in *prayer*, being *watchful* in it with thanksgiving. At the same time, pray also for us, that God may open to us a door for the word, to declare the mystery of Christ . . . that I may make it clear, which is how I ought to speak. Walk in wisdom toward outsiders, making the best use of the time. Let your speech always be gracious, seasoned with salt, so that you may know how you ought to answer each person. (emphasis added)

Philosopher Ludwig Wittgenstein said, "The limits of language means the limits of my world."[3] Are you ready to learn the languages of culture and Christ and enlarge your world? If you can pay attention to culture and participate with Jesus in prayer, you can become bilingual.

Try saying these three sentences out loud:

Jesus loves you.

Love Him back.

Love one another.

I believe you know these statements are true, or you wouldn't have picked up this book. You want your friends and family to understand these words from Jesus as well. I've been waiting for this moment for you. You are not alone in wanting to share your faith. We are a part of the Good News kingdom! Let's learn how to practice the languages of culture and Christ.

Practice.

In every chapter I will give you an actionable idea to practice. I'll also provide some prayers as promptings for your own. I want you to be confident in all your conversations to bring up Christ in a winsome way that enlightens culture. You will become bilingual as you practice paying attention and prayer.

Let's start our practice right now. Who are your people at the gate, the cross, and the table? Write down a few names right here, or somewhere you'll see them often. Think of them as you read this book.

# THE GATE

WE LOVE BECAUSE HE FIRST LOVED US.

1 John 4:19

I was jolted from my work by the sound. There had just been a car accident right outside my house. I didn't see it happen, but I heard the impact and ran out to the intersection in front of my house. I guess I could have chosen to ignore it or leave it to the police or first responders, but we've all got some Good Samaritan in us, no matter our faith. When I arrived, I was shocked to see I knew the driver who was hit, a woman named Lee, who walked out of her car with minor injuries to her hand. Our sons had gone to elementary school together, but that was five years ago. Lee remembered enough about me to recall my beliefs and our vocation, so we caught up on the rest of life while waiting for everything to get reported at the scene. I was able to take care of her hand and give her water and a granola bar. She asked that I call her friend to pick her up, and before she left, I mentioned our church services online that might be encouraging as she rested and healed at home. Over the next few weeks, I checked in on her and sent her and her son food delivery.

This is the gate. We do life with people at the gate because of how much we are all loved by Jesus. Jesus loves me. Jesus loves you. This propels what we do and who we are at the gate. And this truth, alive and at work in and through us, will translate Jesus to others at the gate.

Learn the Language

You and your friend are both Christians. You believe in the same Jesus, yet you vote differently, get your news from different media, have different friends, and engage in different social lifestyles. You both have different church experiences and yet have Christ in common. One of you has little engagement with non-Christians and the other has a world full of them. How can you relate to one another? Do you even understand each other?

You are a Christian and your friend is not. You love the church. She is indifferent to it. You both vote the same and work to raise kind kids. You take your cues from Christ. She takes hers from culture. You have different social lives, different values, and different beliefs, and yet you have local culture in common. Can you be friends? Can you learn from one another?

We are at the gate, the cultural hub, where the language of culture is spoken around us. The gate is where people experiment with everything, where our self-inflicted definitions divide us. Where we go into situations in which we don't agree with one another's political views, parenting style, or poignant remarks, and then we share our unfiltered opinions.

The gate is where we go home for the holidays with a new faith in Jesus and get swallowed up with family values contrary to the Jesus we're following. The family thinks we've lost our mind. We think they have! We're not speaking the same language; we call the other side "confused" and then retreat to our bubble of People Who Get Us.

What if there is a better way? What if we could become bilingual? Let's start by learning what our culture is saying, feeling, and believing in real time by paying attention.

Meet me at Babel.

Humankind began with one language. Genesis 11:1 tells us, "Now the whole world had one language and a common speech" (NIV). Then, in an effort to make a name for themselves, people came together to build something better and higher and greater than God. Ironically, they did this so they could all stay together as one independent human force.

I don't know how far they got or how much they perspired, but in God's kindness and for our sake, He confused humankind. He did this so that we don't put all our earthly efforts into making our names great but rather thrive in His greatness. Our ancestors would shake their heads as humanity continues to say, *Let's make ourselves famous so we won't have to be scattered.* God says, *Scatter and make My name famous.*

God is the reason we have many languages today. This place on the map and moment in history is called the tower of Babel, "because there the LORD confused the language of the whole world" (v. 9 NIV). *Babel* is Hebrew for "confusion." Being thrown into confusion, the people then scattered, not understanding one another fully to this day. Because of our selfishness, we have to work hard to learn each other's languages.

Towers are still being constructed by us today. A famous one is the tower of social media. This is where personal towers get built. Rent is cheap. Megaphones are free. You can buy friends and followers. Post anything without a filter or accountability. Pick and choose from all religious and political views. Scroll and compare your world to others' worlds and expect the same results with apparent ease. When it falls flat, we wonder why it works there but not here. *Hint: it's not the language of the people around you.*

There are other towers at the gate where people work hard to make a name for themselves. The tower of consumerism is being built by what we wear, carry, and possess to determine our status and position in our circles of influence. We build our image by buying the latest, newest, hottest, most up-to-date products, shoes, and clothing. The moment anyone thinks they've made it to the top of the tower of consumerism, the style changes. The tower of labels is adorned with stickers of political parties, sports teams, brands, universities, and more. *Who I know and who I associate with will make my name great. My kid goes to this school. I give to this nonprofit. I am affiliated with this party.* You can't see the tower for all its labels.

God confused our languages back at the tower of Babel, and we're still confused. The devil is at the tower of social media, yet we act shocked that criticism reigns. The devil seeks to disrupt language learning. Theologian John Stott describes the Christian landscape as

strewn with the wreckage of derelict, half-built towers—the ruins of those who began to build and were unable to finish. . . . The

result is the great scandal of so-called nominal Christianity . . .
enough to be respectable, but not enough to be uncomfortable.[1]

We are building ourselves imaginary worlds, making things
sound worse or look better than they really are.

We have other media towers as well. When was the last time
you were able to get clarity from only one news source? We don't
know what is true nor who to believe because we can't understand one another. It's why we go for second opinions and double-
checks. Miscommunication wars and false narratives battle it out
alongside truth, and we're left confused. The media channels have
maxed out their volumes. Has not all humanity become deaf to
every sound except the self-made one on repeat in the quietest
cracks of our day? And what does the self-made one say? It speaks
in a mash-up of whatever voices we have consumed, subconsciously and consciously. Media is a gate to culture but not the
table to community. So how do we approach those at the gate without succumbing to the great tower-building activity present there?

First, we remember God is ahead of all of us. Society will
never get ahead of Him. Look back to the historical tower of
Babel as proof that it's humanly impossible. Yet what is possible
is God revealing Himself to us in creation, science, literature,
and humanity, giving us glimpses of who He is, what He is like,
and what He wants to reveal to us about Himself and His love for
us. Johannes Kepler, a German mathematician and astronomer,
was well known for his three laws of planetary motion. He incor-
porated his belief in God into his work and is known to have said,

I was merely thinking God's thoughts after him. Since we as-
tronomers are priests of the highest God in regard to the book

of nature, it benefits us to be thoughtful, not of the glory of our minds, but rather, above all else, of the glory of God.[2]

Second, we come with our curiosity instead of our building tools. We're not here to build. We don't need a strong tower to draw people to us. We're here to live life at the gate, and also at the cross, and also at the table. Our curiosity helps us learn the language of culture right where we are, a location that varies in its dialect and demographics.

Culture is telling us something.

I don't use rideshares often, though Ben, my husband, does. One Sunday, several of our kids were going early to church so it made more sense for Ben to take them in our van and for me to take a Lyft. My driver, Aaron, picked me up in his Camry, and conversation started immediately about where I was headed. I mentioned church and he went there, both in his car and in conversation. He shared how he put humanity ahead of religion and taught his children to do the same. I shared how the love I get from God affects how I better love humanity. We both agreed that people practice evil in the name of religion, and we wanted no part of it. Then Aaron shifted the conversation as he pointed out an Airbnb billboard on the freeway that read, "Help us host Afghan refugees."

"That's where I'm from," he said. It was a proud and solemn acknowledgment. "I'm overwhelmed with the stressful paperwork of trying to get my parents out of there," he added.

I sympathized with him and asked if I could pray for peace and for his family. He was receptive, and my only request was that he keep his eyes open! "God . . ." I began, for we both believed He existed. I finished praying as we arrived at my church, and I reached into my bag for a church invite card. While I was doing so, he told me that one, no one had ever prayed with him in a rideshare before, and two, he felt an overwhelming peace.

People need Jesus. They hurt. They search. They experiment. They still haven't found what they are looking for. We know this, because only Jesus meets our needs. Why did you say yes to Jesus? What needs of yours does He meet? The humans around us created by God need the gospel and want to experience the love of Christ, so we need to know how to best share it with them. As we become bilingual in the language of Christ, which is prayer, and the language of culture, by paying attention, we can converse successfully about God's love in our present-day contexts.

We don't have to fully understand or agree to be great at listening and caring. If we genuinely care, we will get people's attention. It catches everyone off guard these days. The people at the gate want to experience the love of Jesus, and we can show it to them. Pay attention to needs, patterns, lifestyle choices, and decisions people in your local context are making. As you observe how culture reacts, responds, and receives knowledge and experiences, you will begin to see their longings, pain points, and desires.

Paul wrote to the church in Corinth, "There are doubtless many different languages in the world, and none is without meaning, but if I do not know the meaning of the language, I will be a foreigner to the speaker and the speaker a foreigner to me" (1 Cor. 14:10–11). If we are to be effective disciples of Christ, we've got to learn to listen to our people, the ones who live, work, and breathe beside us.

Jesus knew culture. Yes, He's God, but His people—the Jews (national), the Galileans (regional), and the Nazarenes (local)—raised Him, and He grew up speaking their cultural dialect. In His ministry He used what they were accustomed to and familiar with to engage them. We'll explore in more detail later how Jesus was a listener to His culture, spending time with a divorced woman at a well, a demon-possessed man on the outskirts of town, tax collectors, fishermen, and others at the gate. Also, the apostle Paul didn't walk with Jesus literally and was not one of the original twelve disciples; however, as a missionary, when he got to a place, he paid attention before he began to speak.

We can also be cultural learners. It's not the 1980s. Let us work with intention to stay updated and be cultural learners. That doesn't mean we have to follow culture. It means we learn, are curious, and pay attention.

I suggest you find a bench and people-watch. Put down the phone that supports the towers and observe the people.

What are people doing around you? What do you think is being discussed? How do you perceive they're doing emotionally?

Let's learn culture with the mindset of Christ. When we participate in culture with Christ, we do so without the pressure to alter our standards just because culture does. This is our task: to place the mindset of Christ in front of culture and before any political party and affiliated news channel. If we don't, we will filter Scripture and culture through that lens instead of the reverse.

We learn culture subconsciously through movies we watch, places we go, words we hear, and things we buy. Learning Christ takes more intention. While the twelve disciples learned subconsciously as they lived with Jesus for three years, we have to consciously learn Christ. He's not physically living with us.

We are to seek to understand this world by the light of Jesus so that we can find a piece of common ground with others. It is here we take a moment of their stories, of our shared conversation, and speak a truth. Not just any truth that we grab from the cloud but one that we've personally experienced with God.

Learn the art of double listening.

Not everything we hear is true. I was at an event and therefore had firsthand experience of it, and then I read a newspaper account of it the following day. The harsh reality was that the reporting just wasn't true. We listen so we can hear what culture is also hearing—but we are to double listen.

What does that mean? Pastor and author John Stott coined the term:

> I believe we are called to the difficult and even painful task of "double listening." That is, we are to listen carefully (although of course with differing degrees of respect) both to the ancient Word and to the modern world, in order to relate the one to the other with a combination of fidelity and sensitivity. . . . Only if we can develop our capacity for double listening, will we avoid the opposite pitfalls of unfaithfulness and irrelevance, and be able to speak God's Word to God's world with effectiveness today.[3]

Christ helps us listen to this world and to His Spirit. He is the One and the reason we become bilingual. Let's put double listening into practice using Aaron's story.

What Aaron said: "I'm overwhelmed with all the paperwork."

What he was telling me: "I'm stressed and need peace."

What I heard the Spirit say: "Pray and speak peace over him."

You don't have to be great at sharing your faith to share your faith. You do need to believe Jesus loves you and has called you to love others. Do you believe these truths? You cannot fully be living out these two truths and not be thrust into conversations about Jesus. You have this love from Jesus that others want. This book will lead you into conversations with this truth and your story in order to introduce others to His love.

We practice double listening at the gate, the cross, and the table. This leads to what we say and how we pray. We pay attention to what is being said (culture) but pay even closer attention to what's already been said (God's Word). Jesus loves you. That's a truth to rest in, not a task to accomplish. Let this truth affect how you double listen today.

To those who can speak culture but are learning the language of Christ, consider getting the Spirit's point of view while you're out and about today. Pray, *Holy Spirit, I want to hear from You as I also listen and discern the noise around me.*

Jesus loves you—and this good news is just as much for others as it is for you.

Practice.

Start by paying attention to people around you. If you are unsure about culture but confident in Christ, skip your traditional quiet time today and move it to the coffee shop or a place already on your calendar. Ask God to give you listening ears to those around you.

2 Know the Landscape

We expect culture at the gate. Do we expect Jesus to be there too? What if we believed He's at the gate? If you saw Him there, would it boost your confidence in being there too?

As far as it depends on us as disciples of Christ, let us treat every opportunity on this soil as an opportunity to show His love. Some will only be brief encounters or a seasonal relationship. Others might last a lifetime. Some people will be able to tell our love seems different; others will see it as general acts of kindness. Regardless, let's apply Paul's words here: "Live wisely among those who are not believers, and make the most of every opportunity. Let your conversation be gracious and attractive so that you will have the right response for everyone" (Col. 4:5–6 NLT).

I, for one, want to be trusted by Jesus for the people in my landscape. Landscape is soil. Landscape is the circumstances we find ourselves in on any given day. We can't get a complete perspective from afar or from online. We have to come close. Imagine if God chose to do all He needed to do for us from heaven. How could we relate to such a distant God? How could we expect Him to understand what we go through?

Instead, He chose to come down to us and give us Himself in ways we could experience and more easily grasp.

I urge you to make friends in this world. The languages of culture and Christ are not learned from a program but from practicing with real human beings in real time. Be present. Be attentive. Everywhere you go on every piece of land, whether you call it sacred or secular, belongs to God.

We're in this world daily as disciples of Jesus, on a mission, and He needs to trust us with who He has put around us. We are part of this world; that's not up for debate. We're so enmeshed in it that we don't pay attention to the everyday things going on around us in light of our faith.

You think, *But I'm not up with culture.* Keeping up with culture is exhausting work. However, Jesus teaches us a timeless and winsome approach: we are to be in the world (John 17:18) as His disciples (13:35) with His love entrusted to us to give away (15:12). It's not ultimately how much we know about culture but how we love in our local context. We are to first be in Jesus so we can be Jesus for this world.

Be in the world.

Somehow, and in some distorted way, we've come to accept that the world gets to determine how it is ordered and dictated and experienced. That's far, far from the truth. The world is God's idea. His creation. We are a piece of it. We need to see the world through His eyes, not see Him through the world's eyes. A worldview led by the world will leave us highly disappointed and uninterested. We are to be citizens of both kingdoms—to be in this world but of another world.

How do you know when you're *in* it and when you're *of* it? You can be in a work conversation but not take part in the negative talk and gossip. You can be on a sports team but not take the things other teammates are taking. You can be at a party but not be caught up in the comparison conversations. You can be working from home and hear a crash that beckons you outside instead of only thinking *Not my problem.*

What are some places that come to mind where Jesus spent His time? Well, He walked along the Sea of Galilee—a marketplace for many, because fishing was a major vocation in His culture. He entered people's houses because they invited Him—or He invited Himself! He went to the synagogues to teach, to worship, and, at times, to introduce a better way of living. He took mountain retreats where He and His followers could get rest and perspective from above. Jesus was immersed in His culture because that's where the people were and that's why He came (Luke 19:10). The gate was the whole point of His coming! We miss people at the gate when we assume how Jesus relates to us is how He relates to everyone else. He's so good at meeting us where we're at—and He invites us to do the same with others.

It's not that we hate the world. We love the world. But the world will hate us (John 3:16–20). Christians are called to shine a light on darkness, and it's too much for people to grasp.

What if I had treated Aaron the driver as "in the world" and unapproachable? As if he could only be my rideshare and not a human being made in the image of God who desperately needs peace and help from God? We don't want to escape the culture, for it is our landscape. We don't want to leave the gate, for this is where Jesus wants to be with us, drawing others to Him.

We all have a native tongue. For me, having been at church from birth to this very day, I'm most confident and comfortable with the Christian language. The more time I spend with people in my community, however, the more I learn of its cultural language. When I practice both, I am becoming bilingual.

Be a missionary.

I can recall going on mission trips in the '90s. We would gather all the old Vacation Bible School material we used here in the States, do a refresher on the songs we had motions for, print matching T-shirts, and head off to another country, another culture. I'll speak for myself on this part, but after each mission trip I returned home and went back to my usual routine. Paying attention was for overseas. It was for engaging a very different culture with the love of Christ. Why did I reserve paying attention just for mission trips, just for missionaries? What was I thinking? I missed it. I was a *missing*ary.

A missionary joins in God's love mission for the people and culture. A *missingary* sticks to cultural ways of the sending church or organization and expects the local people to adjust and get on board. I remember driving on the road to Hana, Hawaii, and listening to an audio guide about the history of missionaries to the islands. There were some missionaries who expected the locals to learn to believe like the missionaries believed without taking into account local language, traditions, past, land, or knowledge. Are you a local missionary or missingary?

While Christ followers are to live, walk, and speak differently, we are also to be in touch, love, go, and be with the culture in our context. Nowadays we seek to take discovery trips—to go and observe the culture and seek out ways to be a blessing to the local church in whatever ways are best.

Being on mission is being ready to encourage others with what Christ is doing presently in your life today. A missingary is missing their regular personal and communal time with God, therefore missing opportunities to talk presently. A missionary learns the landscape, establishes trust, and leads with love. A missingary waves their banner, even in the name of Jesus, with little margin for learning and growth.

Allow me to retell a Bible story.

Our Saturday plans were about getting away and finding a place to pray. We were tired from all our traveling, and ministry had been quite time-consuming. We just needed some space to clear our minds and be with God. Interestingly, when you're growing in your confidence in Christ to engage in culture, you never know what you'll get. The landscape was already occupied, so we started conversations with the ladies nearby. One of them was more of a listener than a talker. She did chime in and share what she did for a living and that she had a faith. Paul was one of the guys who was paying attention to where God was leading the conversation, and he made the best use of this opportunity. He shared parts of his story with her, and we watched God open up her heart. We stayed in touch and got to see her whole family come to faith!

Luke's version of this story is found in Acts 16. Though Paul was never called a missionary in the Bible, we know Jesus sent His followers to preach the Good News beyond the Jews and to the gentiles. Some of Paul's encounters were brief, and some happened over his lifetime. Some of our encounters will be brief, like mine with Aaron, while others will intersect over a lifetime.

Paul would visit a place and get to know the landscape before he ever spoke Christ to the people. Many of his letters, which fill many of the pages of our New Testament, show us how to engage with culture appropriately, respectfully, and gracefully. God trusted Paul. His letters to churches are filled with the overflow of the lifelong friendships he established in different cultures.

When you're on mission, you get levels of focus, determination, resilience, and passion that grow with practice.

Think about your day yesterday or today. Where did you go? Who did you see? Not necessarily people you know by name but people you know by location. The people at the store, at the office, around the neighborhood, in the building. What were people doing? Shopping, walking, reading, typing, or eating? Were you doing similar things?

When we pay attention to the circumstances we are in, we have greater potential to be on mission. Either we live on mission or we miss out. And opting to be on mission means you need to be trustworthy for Jesus.

Be trustworthy.

You never know in the landscape if it's a brief encounter or a lifetime friendship. In brief encounters, we say "Hello" and "Take care," provide water, send a meal, show up, and be present. In the long term, we're graced with time and space to listen longer, go deeper, and pick up where we left off the last time. Who are a few people who have been around in your life for a while? I suggest Jesus has a reason for this.

We see this need to be trustworthy in the parable of the talents (Matt. 25:14–30), when the servants who did what was asked could be trusted with more. We also see trustworthiness in the life of Moses (Num. 12:7). Moses could be trusted; God said so. Jesus wants to trust you with what He has already generously given you. He wants to trust you to raise your children well, to take care of strangers, to love one another, to go and make disciples. Christ wants to trust us to lead people into truth, not being weird about it but being winsome for His sake and glory.

We must discuss *weird*, because either we are that awkward Christian or we've experienced weird Christianity and cringe when we see it. We can avoid this as Christ followers by learning the languages of both culture and Christ. Weird happens when we try too hard to fit in with culture or when we are insensitive about what we bring to culture concerning Christianity.

Imagine a world and nation where we lived only with Christians and did life only with Christians and listened only to Christian music and ate only at Christian restaurants and went only on Christian vacations and worked only for Christian companies and went only to Christian schools and supported only Christian nonprofits. We would look at any other group and call it cultish. We would call it weird.

The message of Jesus is for both Jew and gentile. The people of Israel who thought Jesus was coming just for them got it wrong. He came for every person who would ever live. If your beliefs are for only a certain group of people, you belong to a cult, not Christianity.

This is the high call of Christ: to live a godly life among people who have yet to follow Jesus. Do this and people will see Jesus. Scripture does tell us to avoid certain people, but I believe we're to avoid their influence, not avoid them altogether. Let's be the kind of people Paul wrote to Timothy about—those who obey Jesus (2 Tim. 3:1–5, 14–17). Jesus is looking for people whose eyes are fixed on Him, who are living lives of trust in Him. He can trust those people with more.

Practice.

Pause for a moment today when you are at work, in the marketplace, or around town. Remind yourself Jesus is in you in your world.

3 Meet the People

If we only talk Jesus to Jesus people, we won't know who doesn't know. Jesus said, "And if you greet only your own people, what are you doing more than others?" (Matt. 5:47 NIV). He told us to go and make disciples. You have permission to be among culture even if your Christian friends question you. You need non-Christian friends in your life. They are some of the kindest, most brilliant people on the planet. If non-Christians are your only friends, I'll address having Christian community in the next section. For now, let's pay attention and meet someone.

Maybe you need to reengage with culture. Over time, perhaps inadvertently, you've isolated from society and insulated yourself in the church. You don't spend time at the gate because the cross keeps you busy. Yet you can't become bilingual if you're only working on one language. We're going where we're going at the gate in the name of Jesus, not just to shop and eat and get what we need but to make the marketplace a better place.

So let me ask, Do you love people? I'm not talking about tolerating them. When you stop and think about it, do you truly love others, and when you push everything that's different about them aside, do you long for them to know and experience the love of Jesus that has changed your life? Let us take hold of the words of Michael Ramsey, the archbishop of Canterbury in the 1960s: "We state and commend the faith only in so far as we go out and put ourselves inside the doubts of the doubters, the questions of the questioners and the loneliness of those who have lost their way."[1]

I want you to meet someone.

My name is Charleston, actually.

I had just started sliding hangers to the left when a large man wearing many layers appeared to my right. He brushed up against me then quickly apologized and got back to what he was doing. *What was he doing?* The second the question rose in me, so did fear. He was arranging store goods into his layers, his back very close to my right side. Just as I realized this, my eyes spotted a beautiful light gray velvet dress with a red sticker on top of the price tag. Who else loves red stickers?

My hands seemed to move in slow motion for the dress on the rack. My brain lost communication with my feet. My palms grew wet. My body temperature rose. Something in my spirit said, *Tell him Jesus loves him. Tap him on the shoulder. Tell him Jesus loves him.*

I knew this was why my feet wouldn't move. My body wasn't running because the Holy Spirit had work to do right there. Most times I know when it's the Holy Spirit prompting me because it's something I wouldn't naturally choose to do on my own. Can you identify?

I tapped his shoulder, and whispered just loud enough for the two of us to hear, "Sir, I don't know what you're going through, but I'm supposed to tell you that Jesus loves you. He loves you very much."

He pivoted to look at me for several seconds. "Thank you," he said.

It was the most sincere thank-you I have ever received. The next moment an employee came over and asked him if he needed a basket for his items. I loved her question! There was no shame or accusation in her posture. I also loved that my feet came unlocked, my hands were able to reach for the velvet dress with the red sticker, and I took it straight to the dressing room. It fit perfectly, and I attributed that to the calories I'd burned in all the right places in the previous moment.

I needed to pay for the dress and then hustle out of the store to get to a meeting. *I'll process this all later*, I told myself. But the man with layers was waiting for me. *Don't think scary. Think God. Think "I can't make this stuff up." Think about being caught up in something that I'll try to retell one day. Think that!*

He said, "I'm not doing good. I'm in a really bad place. You reminding me that Jesus loves me is what I need to hear."

Here we were again. Me, the man, and the Holy Spirit.

"What's your name?" I asked.

"Charles. Charleston, actually."

"I'm Shauna." We shook hands. "Charleston, I meant it. Jesus does love you. I had the hardest time getting those words out to you though," I told him.

He looked surprised. Neither of us knew much about one another. We could make guesses—no, we had already made guesses—about each other. We talked a little. I told him I'd found a place where I could feel loved and accepted and learn about Jesus. I handed him a church invite card, pointed in the direction of our church, and invited him to come. He smiled, looked interested, and walked away.

My work wasn't over. I thought I saw the employee who'd brought Charleston the basket. Her name was Maggie, and I asked her if she was the one who approached us earlier, as if Charleston and I had been working as a team.

"Yes, and because of what you said to him, he emptied our store goods from his layers into the basket," she said.

How did she know what I'd said? While I was in the dressing room, Charleston told Maggie that I'd told him Jesus loves him. And she told him that it was true! It was now Maggie's turn to see the Holy Spirit at work. I asked if she believed in God, and she said yes. And guess what? She was also the store manager! The Holy Spirit used Maggie and me that weekday. She was on the clock. I was in between meetings. Charleston was right where he needed to be to hear the truth that Jesus loves him. He wasn't at church. He was attempting to shoplift at a Marshalls. This is why it matters that we learn to speak the language of culture and Christ. When we're prayerful and attentive, we can participate in the Spirit's activity in our local contexts every single day of the week.

What's your name?

We all know that person. We give them a double take, hold our belongings tighter, and walk on the other side of the street, avoiding them entirely. They're not in their right mind. They could hurt us. Something about them is off.

The people of the land that is now modern-day Syria knew that person too. He was naked and homeless. Local authorities had tried every kind of restraint on this man. When he was demon possessed, he preferred to live away and alone among the tombs. Honestly, the people preferred it that way too.

"What's your name?" Jesus asked him.

"Legion."

"Out with you all."

The more I read Mark's account of this story, the more I'm convinced Jesus eventually called the man by the name given by his momma. It's just that the man was so overcome by demons, he didn't even know his own name. It would be just like Jesus to ask him again after he was released and set free. Not because Jesus didn't know it, but hearing our names isn't a head thing, it's a heart thing. We hear our names with our hearts.

"Now, what's *your* name?" I can hear Jesus say.

When I asked Charleston his name, he initially said Charles because that's what people called him today. But then he dug deeper and found his identity.

"Charleston, actually," he said. "That's what my grandmother named me."

He went back to love. Back to family. Back to the start.

What did your momma or grandma call you at birth? Who does God say you are? If you've never been told, or you've forgotten, God calls you beloved (Rom. 9:25). You are wonderfully made (Ps. 139:14). Jesus calls you friend (John 15:15) and blessed (Eph. 1:3). He says you are chosen and forgiven (1:4, 7). This is also who God says Aaron, Lee, and Charleston are.

Learning names is meeting people. Upon first impression, you might initially meet doubt, depression, disgust, or disillusionment before you learn their name. If they wear a name tag because of their job, that's a bonus! Call them by their name.

When you learn their name, you get to the heart, and then "Jesus loves you" starts to matter. That day in Marshalls I met a non-Christian and I got to share how much Jesus loves him, and in doing so, I was reminded how much He loves me too. "Jesus loves you" is for all of us.

Jesus loves you.

The language of Jesus is the language of love. The devil's language is lies. There are unspoken languages in culture, but they are seldom unheard. In learning the language of culture, paying attention by double listening often uses actions rather than words.

We got a thank-you card from our neighbor Marie, whom we had met the night before as we handed out popcorn during the pandemic. I want my life to reach the Maries, and I can only do that by being at the gate, ready to double listen. Ready to convey, in spoken or unspoken ways, that Jesus loves them.

People are seeking, even though they may not know how to go about it. And the simple truth that Jesus loves us is just too simple for people. Perhaps it's easier to believe He can love other people, but not us. We're so close to our own hearts we hear the broken pieces, and we feel embarrassed by our thoughts.

Jesus speaks to pain, isolation, and torment, and He also speaks to impure spirits. The reason Jesus came to earth was to destroy the works of the devil and to replace lies with truth (1 John 3:8). He's speaking that to you and to those you meet at the gate. He also came so that we might live through him (4:9) and love because He first loved us (v. 19). The love of the Father is so profound. Even if people can't get their minds around all the other stuff, we all want to be loved, and loved unconditionally.

Let love be our motivation. We don't get prizes or eternal wealth if someone comes to trust in Jesus. We get more. He has changed my life, and He's still changing my life! We get freedom, and we can share it. The world's definition of *love* is circumstantial, provisional, and comes with exceptions. It is weak and lacking. But not so with God's love. Read 1 John 3:14, and you'll see it is all about God's love and our love for one another.

If you only see people like you, you'll miss out on the diversity of the kingdom of God, and heaven will be culture shock. It begins as a quiet operation of listening to your people.

When have you seen a fisherman sitting on the shore just waiting for fish to jump out of the water and land next to him? When Jesus called His followers to be "fishers of men," that came with an obvious expectation that we would seek people out. He said, "I will *make* you fishers of men" (Matt. 4:19, emphasis added). Yes, some have the gift of evangelism and seem more confident because of what flows naturally, but we all have to learn this as disciples of Christ. I don't have the natural gift of cooking, but I must cook to feed my family. I don't have the natural gift of interior design, but I do want some things on our walls at home. With practice, I can become a better cook. By learning from others, I can develop more of an eye for design.

Jesus uses the same word in his final moment on earth: "Go and *make* disciples" (Matt. 28:19 NIV, emphasis added). We—the church and Christians and whomever else you want to put in this category—have made it so complicated. Jesus said to follow Him, and He'll make us what we can't be on our own. Follow Jesus to observe the cultural landscape, to engage with the culture. He spent time at the gate. It's time we do too.

Practice.

- Who are your non-Christian friends? Make some. Your life and faith will be better for it.
- If you have some, and they came to the place you worship on Sunday, would they call it a church or a cult? Attach yourself to a church your non-Christian friends will be welcomed to.
- What are their values, idols, patterns, and interests? Start with observation, but then move on to conversation. Observation gets you far; conversation will get you further.
- What is the latest worldview or cultural theory you've been exposed to? Keep learning with discernment.
- What is a current pop-culture trend you've learned about? Go engage with it.

4 Listen to Stories

You think you can't relate to the ever-changing culture, but you can listen. Yet listening takes time, and time is a precious commodity we run out of before it even arrives. As disciples of Jesus, we need to listen to find common ground. We listen for *me too* moments. Hearing someone else say *me too* communicates "You see me and get a piece of me." We listen to understand. If we listen, everything said can be traced back to God, and He works magic! He doesn't really, and neither does coffee (more on that in a bit), but if you have seen the works of God, then you know what He does is supernatural.

We also listen to ask questions, to ask for definitions, to ask for clarity—and then we listen more. My favorite people in life are the ones who really listen to me rather than always talk at me. Is that also true for you?

A 1957 study by Ralph G. Nichols and Leonard A. Stevens published by *Harvard Business Review* continues to be circulated. They concluded,

When we listen, we ask our brain to receive words at an extremely slow pace compared with its capabilities. . . . When we listen, therefore, we continue thinking at high speed while the spoken words arrive at low speed. . . . To phrase it another way, we can listen and still have some spare time for thinking. . . .

The newspapers reported not too long ago that a church was torn down in Europe and shipped stone by stone to America, where it was reassembled in its original form. The moving of the church is analogous to what happens when a person speaks and is understood by a listener. The talker has a thought. To transmit his thought, he takes it apart by putting it into words. The words, sent through the air to the listener, must then be mentally reassembled into the original thought if they are to be thoroughly understood. But most people do not know what to listen for, and so cannot reconstruct the thought.[1]

Jesus, who continues to be the greatest listener of all time, said this: "Consider carefully how you listen. Whoever has will be given more; whoever does not have, even what they think they have will be taken from them" (Luke 8:18 NIV).

If you don't say anything, it can't be heard. Only thinking about your friend who doesn't know Jesus helps no one. This is why we learn the language of culture and Christ to become bilingual in order to translate Jesus. Listening to stories is what makes coffee magic, listening an art, and questions the best conversational tool we've been given.

Coffee is magic.

Coffee works its magic simply by giving us something to hold in our hands to keep us from being awkward. Let it be an excuse to really listen. Places we go to enjoy our drink of choice are neutral ground. The well was this kind of place in New Testament times, as was the sea—places people felt were familiar, comfortable, and regular. Church will always bring up a correlation for many with having to be cleaned up and put together in order to enter one. That's why church isn't often the first point of connection with people.

I continue to make my case for the gate being a powerful entry point to people. Consider the following five conversations.

Christine and I ordered our coffee at the walk-up window at Piccino's in the Dogpatch neighborhood of our city. We stepped back and waited for the barista to do her magic, then we found chairs in the park and dragged them to a sunny spot for continued conversation. Christine picked up where we had left off. She laughed as she recalled hearing about Jesus at age seven and thinking the description sounded more like an alien. She shared her Taiwanese upbringing on the East Coast and her parents' expectation that she become a doctor. I could hear that these lifelong expectations continued to dominate Christine's everyday decisions and were the very reason she held back on exercising faith due to logic. But holding that magical cup of coffee slowed me down and kept my mouth closed and my ears percolating for more.

Tiffany learned about Jesus in her childhood, but it was her boyfriend who brought her back to church. She began to see that Jesus just might be what was missing in her life. She joined a Bible study, and periodically we'd meet at the park during lunch. Pulling back the wrap of my magical sandwich, I would listen as Tiffany told me how she was strategically trying to fit Jesus into her decisions, work, and relationships.

My guys were playing volleyball in the pool on our first day of family vacation in Cancun with several others, and I made small talk with Adrianne and Summer, a mom and sister of their own volleyball players. This small talk included names and ages of kids, where we lived, and what we did. With a magical fruity drink of the virgin variety, Summer approached me to tell me more of her story and ask for more of ours.

The flight attendant asked what we wanted to drink, and since Coca-Cola tastes better thirty thousand feet up, I went for it. Dion, in the seat next to me, did the same. This interlude created space for us to share about where we were going and where we were coming from. His final destination was far more exotic than mine, but our starting points were both in San Francisco. As I sipped my carbonated magic, he pointed out the book I was reading and said he read the same one. He even took it with him to work, and it got him through the hardest of days.

Nino, Nikole, and Alli came from all over the world to study at a university in the city. Though they were only here for a semester, I learned about their cultures and pursuits of their dreams, often over a free meal our church offered every Tuesday evening. Once, over a magical cup of chai, they shared their doubts and questions, and we laughed in awe about how God works and how they had been to church more in three months than in their nineteen years of life.

To listen, you have to start with what you hear. I hear the steam from the espresso machine. I listen to Christine's childhood. I hear the surround-sound of people walking through the park. I listen to Tiffany process out loud. I hear the lulling muffle of the airplane engine. I listen to Dion's history in the city. It's not until I listen to the people that I can begin to learn and practice the language of culture. Hearing is a necessary first step, but it's not the last step.

Hearing is a sense. Listening is concentration. Hearing is easy. Listening is a skill. The learned art of listening develops the discipline of focus. Practice by listening to a song, all of it. We hear lots of things. The question for us at the gate: Are we listening to what culture is telling us, or just hearing?

In his book *Contemporary Christian*, John Stott shares this powerful thought:

> Unless we listen attentively to the voices of secular society, struggle to understand them, and feel with people in their frustration, anger, bewilderment and despair, weeping with those who weep, we will lack authenticity as the disciples of Jesus of Nazareth. Instead we run the risk (as has often been said) of answering questions no one is asking, scratching where nobody is itching, supplying good for which there is no demand.[2]

So let's ask ourselves again, Are we listening to what culture is telling us?

Everyone has a gospel.

Everyone is holding on to some good news, whether they are living for the moment or have something or someone they can depend upon to be good. Listen for their gospel. Listen for what they look to and hold to in hard times, then ask about their everyday reality. Then listen some more. As a way of connecting with culture, ask yourself, *What good news did I hold on to before I put my hope in the Good News of Jesus?*

Often when we hear something contrary to what we believe, a mental rebuttal forms in our minds. When this happens, we stop listening to understand and start listening to fire away. We miss half of the conversation because as the other person is talking, we are drawing conclusions, building up our walls, making assumptions, passing judgment, and determining their fate.

God, give us ears to hear and eyes to see.

Understanding one another doesn't mean we see things the same way. Someone reading this chapter won't like me using the word *magic*, as if I've just cast a spell. To me, magic has sparkles and conjures up childlike wonder. There I go again, conjuring up mixed feelings. Someone will offend me when they take God's name in vain. I will raise my voice for the unborn and women's health and human love. I seek not to upset or offend but to listen for common language so I can understand others. At times, this does mean I can understand how others see things the way they do. I can see why they chose that school for their child, though I wouldn't choose it for mine. I can see why they support that cause, although it's not that important to me. They can understand why I go to church every Sunday, even though they spend the day differently.

Are you listening to understand, or are you listening to be ready to speak and defend? If you listen to understand, there are times you will need to say, "I don't see it that way, but I'm glad you shared that with me." Or "I don't see the point of that show / the value in that goal / the purpose of that organization, but I'm glad you shared it with me." Or perhaps they don't observe what you observe, teach what you teach, or support the organization you support, but they made space for you to share with them.

Gen Zers, for example, prefer Christians to approach them by listening without judgment, according to Barna Research. This was the highest characteristic for both non-Christian and Christian Gen Zers.[3] You can say when they are done talking, "So what I hear you say is . . ." and repeat back to them their words.

> While listening, the main object is to comprehend each point made by the talker. Judgments and decisions should be reserved until after the talker has finished. At that time, and only then, review his main ideas and assess them.[4]

Listening and engaging with respect are easier desired than accomplished. Nevertheless, we keep on practicing. We don't force a conclusion. For example, one day an acquaintance sought me out through email. She treated me to a magical cup of coffee. What took intention on my part was to show up and listen. We didn't close the conversation but left it open for next time and for more thinking. We don't see the world the same way. We believe in different gospels and speak different languages. Winn Collier, a pastor who continues to teach me through his books, wrote, "There can be no language that works at all if someone is not listening. And since God is the primary voice in this gospel world, we [pastors] have to lead the way in listening, doing it ourselves and encouraging others to do it."[5]

Talk to them about them.

I've watched Ben do this well for years. He listens to ask questions. He keeps the questions going based on what he's heard from the individual.

According to Gary Keller in *The One Thing*, "Asking questions increases learning by 150%."[6] Let this be a statistic synonymous with Christ's disciples. God gave us two ears and one mouth. Ask people about their beliefs, their family, their values. Listen to what they say.

As you listen, pay attention to what Jesus is doing around this person even if they don't recognize Him yet. If they speak of pain, where do you see Jesus trying to comfort them? If they open up about their unhealthy habits, what is a healthy area God is drawing them into? If they talk about tough relationships, what truths is God bringing to your mind to share that will bring them hope?

"I hear you say [repeat back what you heard]."

"Help me understand . . ."

"Where did this idea or truth you hold to come from?"

Then listen more.

Let's not listen because we've got something to say. Let's not pull the Christian card and let them go first because we know we'll go next and go longer. Let's not listen to convert but listen unconditionally, expecting not to say a thing. The genuine love of Jesus is best visible in us, His followers, when we listen to people's stories. Everyone wants to be loved and cared for, and that takes our time. Show you care. Your friend will know. Trust me. A fraud is easier to detect than we think. Let Jesus be visible in your kindness and listening and time.

The world and culture can only listen from a place of mindfulness. Christians have the Spirit of the living God connecting our mind, soul, will, and emotions to enable us to be holistic listeners. In becoming bilingual, in translating Jesus, mindfulness bears a supernatural component having to do with an awareness of God, others, and ourselves. And in that order.

When you look at all of society, when you look at your local context, when you look at people in your sphere of influence, do you believe the Jesus of the Bible—the Jesus you are trusting in for eternity—can heal and forgive? Do you believe He has risen, defeated death, and is returning?

As disciples of Jesus, we must have time to listen, to reflect, to ask questions. I know, crazy, huh? The hardest thing we all experience in our days is running out of time. We are a pitied society to be given twenty-four hours a day and using them up on non-eternal objects and projects.

The world does a great job of asking us questions. Christ followers must do the same.

Why do you believe what you believe?

What were you taught as a child?

When tragedy or trials come, how do you cope?

What motivates you and inspires you? What's behind that motivation/inspiration?

What's the basis for your decision-making?

Why do you teach that?

What do those lyrics do to your heart?

How does that show affect your life?

Jesus, who taught His followers with authority, said, "Everyone who hears these words of mine and puts them into practice is [wise]. . . . But everyone who hears these words of mine and does not put them into practice is [foolish]" (Matt. 7:24, 26 NIV). Let's put His words into practice. If we follow Him, so much will be taken care of.

Practice.

Genuinely practice saying, "Me too," as you listen so you can relate. And the next time you ask a question, listen only for the answer.

5 Practice the Language

I was eight years old, and I was glad! I understood it as best I could: Jesus was for me, not against me. He not only created me but had my days numbered, so I could trust Him with my life. My childhood record was fairly clean, though I had some mean thoughts here and some lies there and some stolen erasers in my Caboodle for popularity points. On my own, I could not keep myself from thinking wrong, doing wrong, or having the eraser theft be the first of many. I needed help from Someone who was perfect; though He had been tempted in every way, He was without sin (Heb. 4:15). Someone who thought I was worth it to come down and die for my sins, so I didn't have to—all out of love.

This one act on the cross saved me. Jesus then beat death, came back to life, and left His Spirit to guide me and you today. This is the Good News. This is the gospel. This is my hope. This gives me purpose.

And yet I forget. I take what Jesus has done for me for granted. I live spoiled as I go through my day with the most precious gift of salvation tucked away for the afterlife. I appreciate what He has done for me, but not enough to change.

This is not Christianity—when we take the free gift of salvation and eternal life for ourselves and do not let it change us to the point of sharing it with others. If Christ hasn't changed our lives, we certainly won't want to spend all of eternity with Him or bring anyone else along. We will not care if others know Jesus if we have forgotten Him. We will not care if others find Jesus if we have lost our love for Him.

But if He has changed your life, then you are grateful today that Jesus loves someone like you, can forgive someone like you, and has died for you. You've got a story to tell simply because you're living a life that has been changed by Him.

Remember your story.

Remember when you said yes to Jesus. Remember His incredible love for you. Take your time. If you rush past this, you'll also rush past others. I'm looking around a coffee shop as I remember my story. Jesus came for every person in here. Every one of us is His unique creation. The man with the Yankees hat and the ladies catching up on life. The two men on their construction work break. The student with her stacks of textbooks. And I remember. I remember Jesus is love. I remember His death and resurrection have made a way for us to know Him. I remember if He can forgive, so can I. I remember if He loves me so much, I can take that love and give it away. Who comes to your mind? Who do you see?

Seth drives on 6th Street and remembers. He sees a city that Jesus died for, and that reminds him he can give his life for those who live here. Collette is surprised by the ingratitude of a beggar when she gives him a coffee gift card. In seeing his brokenness, she is reminded of the brokenness in her life that Jesus has mended.

Are you remembering? I hope so, because your story is needed wherever you go. Who Jesus is and what He has done for you keeps you grounded as you engage with your people. Be confident in it. Use it often, not always with words but in remembering. For in remembering, you obey.

King David needed reminding. He prayed, "Restore to me the joy of your salvation and grant me a willing spirit, to sustain me" (Ps. 51:12 NIV). Make that your prayer: "Jesus, give me back the joy that comes from knowing You as my Savior and Lord and make me willing to obey You."

The wonder of remembering reconnects us with Jesus. Then we connect with our story, because everything Jesus does is personal. Wherever Jesus found you and whatever it took for you to recognize His love is what makes your story special. All of our stories are in process, and you can share parts of yours and listen for common language.

Talk to your people about Jesus.

We don't need to wait until we're fluent in the language of Beth Moore or Maverick City Music or the translators of the King James Bible. I just spoke with Pete, who is in town visiting his hundred-year-old dad. Within five minutes, we covered the election, his high school alma mater, and his English essay, which was inspired by helping a drunk man on a street corner he can point to outside the coffee shop window. I gave him my email address as a small gesture if he needed us to take his father anything or to check in on him after Pete returned home to Florida.

What I didn't say was, "Hey, I'm a Christian. This is what good churchgoing Christians do. Do you know Jesus? I've heard you use His name a time or two, but incorrectly." Rather, I told him we live far from family too, and it means so much to have people here we can call on in time of need. He asked what I was working on. It was then I got to tell him I was writing this book for disciples of Jesus to practice the language of Christ and culture.

I didn't tell him my eight-year-old's salvation story, though I am living on that foundation. Our stories are made to grow, to include the continuing work of the Holy Spirit, who is refining us and changing us into His image. We are to add to our faith virtue, knowledge, self-control, steadfastness, godliness, brotherly affection, and love, says the apostle Peter (2 Pet. 1:3–7). Let these qualities be always forming in you. This keeps you effective and fruitful (v. 8). If they are not active in your life, it's because you have forgotten what Jesus did for you (v. 9). "For if you practice these qualities you will never fall" and you will have "an entrance into the eternal kingdom of our Lord and Savior Jesus Christ" (vv. 10–11).

The key for translating Jesus is practice. We will continue to work on our stories at the cross and the table. No matter what you've believed before, reconnecting with your Jesus story is necessary to connect with others' stories at the gate. **When I started believing this, I stopped being intimidated by the culture I live in and started becoming influenced by Jesus.**

We never know how God will use us in the lives of strangers, but it's our directive as Christ taught in Matthew 25 to minister to those who can't necessarily minister back to us in the same way. What if, in your giving a cup of water, an unexpected friendship forms? What if vulnerably sharing your faith story leads to more? What if God transforms the conversations you have regularly with another family at the park into a friendship around the table? It's not up to us to know; it's up to us to say hello. Talking to strangers is like exercise. If you don't do it enough, you fall out of practice. Smartphones and the formative effects of the COVID global pandemic have also caused us not to have in-person conversations. We've forgotten or don't know how to dialogue or talk to strangers, so it's time to practice.

Eugene Peterson, at a similar conflicting point with his people, wrote,

> I reflected on what I was doing when they didn't see me. I reflected on what they were doing when I didn't see them. I wrote it [in a newsletter] every Tuesday. The church secretaries mailed it out every Wednesday. A deliberate use of language to connect Sunday language with weekday language.[1]

That was his solution. But there's no script for this, only cues in unexpected spaces.

Take cues from the shepherds.

They peered in with a little more faith than fear remaining from their enlightening moment in the field.

"May we come in?"

"This is an odd question, but was a baby born in here tonight?"

"So, um, well, this messenger showed up and . . . oh, an angel spoke to you too?"

Joseph and Mary and the shepherds swapped stories as they marveled at this experience with the God-child. After some time, they turned their attention to outside the stable.

We believe all of this, but will they?

It quickly went from angel to shepherd to beholding Jesus! Angels were the initial messengers chosen to break the four hundred years of silence since the prophets to Joseph, Mary, Zechariah, and the shepherds.

They said they were bringing good news of the great joy variety. It would be for everybody, and they'd get the message, but presently the news was for the shepherds. As in, *it's happening right now.*

If the shepherds had been told to go to a hotel or castle, they would have second-guessed it, but a stable was their turf. God's messenger was speaking their language! God used the familiar landscape, yet He also ushered in the supernatural that wowed them. He is familiar with your landscape and is ushering in this same supernatural to wow you and your people as well.

Luke says of the shepherds, "And when they saw it, they made known" (2:17). We tell what we know. We tell what we've seen.

See. Make known. Then let wonder do its work. Let go of control and timelines. Let your people wonder.

"All who heard it wondered at what the shepherds told them" (v. 18). Of course they wondered. This message didn't make sense upon first hearing. What the shepherds shared didn't add up. *It's been nothing but silence; now you want us to believe* what? It would have been twenty generations since they'd heard the prophets. Stories passed down would have lost their luster or buried the faith. Do we give space and grace for people to wonder?

Let us take our cue from the shepherds. They simply responded to the gospel. It was too good not to consider its truth. Whatever excuse holds you back from speaking of your faith is crushed right now in the name of Jesus. If Jesus is the Good News, if He has changed your life, if He is who you are trusting for your eternity, if He saved you, if He is who you model your life after, pray to, want to grow in, follow, and obey, then drop any excuse for not translating Jesus.

The shepherds shared what they knew. They shared what they had. We want there to be good news, but good news needs a shepherd to share it. This first message didn't come from the top down but from the down up. I imagine the shepherds present for Christ's birth were also at the cross because of what they encountered out in the fields and especially at the stable. I believe they never missed a moment!

"And the shepherds returned," according to Luke 2:20. They went back to work, back to their regular routine. Differently, of course! I believe they were Christ's earliest followers and kept up-to-date with His life all the way to the cross. Just as the shepherds didn't need to give up their day jobs (or night jobs) to share their stories, your vocation and purpose are crucial to becoming bilingual.

The world of the shepherds was personal and local. They didn't have to go far, yet the message would travel far. Good news travels fast! It flows out of our own relationships. And the gospel of Jesus is factual, so be confident in telling it. The shepherds learned of and shared the Good News in real time for them. It's in real time for us too. Share it and let it sink in. The power of good news is it keeps being retold. Even for people who think and ponder like Mary did, if it makes its way into hearts and minds, something else will trigger it again!

Let us learn to be patient with continuing stories and trust that God will bring people to carry on what we get to be a part of. In his book *The Deeply Formed Life,* my friend Rich Villodas wrote, "The more we create spaces for people who don't look like us, think like us, or believe like us, the more we will be able to introduce them to Jesus."[2]

The times we mess up on delivering good news are when we don't trust that the news itself will transform others, though it did for us. Pratyush Buddiga was riding the school bus in middle school when another student told him if he didn't believe in Jesus he would burn in hell. Prat went on to spell *prospicience* correctly and became the 75th Scripps National Spelling Bee Champion. He was living the good and successful American dream and had forgotten all about that kid's claim on the bus. It wasn't until after he'd secured the #2 spot in the global poker rankings that he hit rock bottom. Prat was working his way up from this low point while in Singapore and, while on a date to a Christian concert, he learned that Jesus loved him, and this truth encounter changed everything for Prat. His date, Gwen, became his wife. Jesus became his everything. Today, they are practicing the language of culture where they live and in their vocations; they are listening for common language among friends, family, and colleagues to introduce Jesus.

Take your cues from the shepherds, not the kid on the bus. It's not how much you know to believe but that you've experienced His love, and out of the overflow you tell others.

Practice.

Stick to what Jesus has done in your life up to this present moment, for no one can argue your story.

6 Read the Scriptures

Do you think your words today could save someone's life?

Because the Scriptures are alive, they come off the page, into your soul, and are active in you. This reality changes what happens at the gate and who's present at the gate, and it grows a company of enthusiastic witnesses. We can live in such a way as Christians that miracles happen at the gate like they did for Jesus. Luke 7:12 tells of Jesus resurrecting a boy at a literal gate. We don't have to get people to an event at church for them to hear the Good News.

Scripture is crucial to translating Jesus and will be needed at the gate, the cross, and the table. I suggest that people who read the Bible run a higher risk of being transformed by Jesus. It did so for Stephen.

A diverse and, at the time, global crowd was giving keen interest to this discipleship model of preaching the Word and serving the community. Stephen was a justice guy, known around town for serving tables and caring for widows. His work took place Monday through Saturday.

It's not like Stephen rehearsed what he read in the Scriptures in front of the mirror with a foreshadowing thought that he would soon give a historic speech and breathe his last. Meditating on the Holy Scriptures was just what he did. He had women in town depending on his ministry to provide them with a warm meal and some groceries that day. But he was no fool. Tensions were mounting, and he knew everything he did was under careful watch by the self-proclaimed leaders of the law who made no room for Jesus. Stephen prayed daily for those he served and those who hated him. Both numbers seemed to be growing.

What happens at the gate doesn't stay at the gate.

And Stephen, full of grace and power, was doing great wonders and signs among the people. Then some of those who belonged to the synagogue of the Freedman (as it was called), and of the Cyrenians, and of the Alexandrians, and of those from Cilicia and Asia, rose up and disputed with Stephen. (Acts 6:8–9)

The movement was also growing. Its early disciples went from "increasing in number" to "being multiplied" because everyone was pleased to be doing their part as either preachers or servers. Stephen was of the serving category, but notice this didn't keep him from preaching. You might be in corporate work, but God wants to speak through you as you serve. You might be in full-time ministry, but God wants to serve through your hands and not just your lips. Stephen was doing wonders at the gate in his place of service, which was his weekday ministry among the people, and some didn't like it. Oddly enough, these leaders of the law twisted Stephen's words as he shared truths from Scripture, writings they supposedly all read and followed.

Reading the Bible affects how you see and relate to others. It did for Stephen. It affected how he served and how he spoke. I suppose that these religious leaders were lying. They weren't really reading the Scriptures, for if they were, they would have been changed by them and not have taken Stephen down. When these leaders could not speak with the same Spirit and from the same Scriptures, they conjured up a false narrative and drew in people susceptible to believing anything they said because of who they were.

Stephen explained the history of how the people got to where they were living, tracing it back to Abraham (7:2–8). He referred to their forebears because he was one of them and because they were familiar with this history. Truth can outrage us, because to us it's more outrage than truth. Think of a matter that can make you mad merely upon hearing the subject. An elected official's views. An issue on an upcoming ballot. A neighbor's habits. How an organization handled a situation. A coworker's sly skills. A mandate enforced at work.

The leaders of the law grew more upset after hearing Stephen share Moses's story. Moses's story! How can this be? Stephen had the Old Testament as his guide and Moses as a historical figure who did signs and wonders. Acts 7:22 says, "Moses was educated in all the wisdom of the Egyptians and was powerful in speech and action" (NIV). Stephen went to the Old Testament to draw a parallel with the moment at hand. He reminded them, "Moses thought that his own people would realize that God was using him to rescue them, but they did not" (v. 25 NIV).

No one argued that Moses was a hero, a saint of his time. Stephen recounted how Moses tried a ministry of reconciliation with two people at his gate, but they shamed and questioned him, so Moses ran far away, lived as an exile, and started a family (vv. 26–29). Then God called Moses back.

God is calling you back too. Back to the gate, back to the very people who outrage you and those who don't get your Jesus life.

"This Moses . . . this man . . . this is the Moses . . . this is the one." The same Moses they had rejected. God wants to use the same *us* too. Not a different us. "He was sent to be their ruler and deliverer by God himself . . . and he received living words to pass on to us" (vv. 35, 38 NIV). Still, people refused and rejected him. Not all people received Moses. They weren't receiving Stephen either.

Not everyone will receive you, but there are a few in your life who are paying attention. What happens at the gate doesn't stay at the gate for this very reason.

Reading the Scriptures accomplishes God's purpose in the reader. The prophet Isaiah ties reading Scripture to the result of joy. When Philip shared Jesus in Acts 8:8, his translations led to great joy in the city. Reading the Scriptures transformed Stephen's life. God's truth got into him, and that's what he spoke of when called into question, when asked to speak truth. He didn't just quote Scripture; he translated the biblical text to the people to whom he was speaking. He made it personal. He used contrast and comparison to paint a relevant picture.

If God's Word doesn't return to Him empty (Isa. 55:11), that includes His Word in you. Read well and read often.

- Read or listen to the Bible to see what God is up to, for we are still living in New Testament times. The events in Revelation haven't happened. We're not living on the other side of the Bible quite yet.

- Read or listen to the Bible, because this is how God speaks to you.

Pay attention to what's already been said in the Bible—and yes, pay attention to what's being said in culture. Your life speaks at the gate. Your weekday stories and discipleship teach. Don't rule anyone out. Be sensitive and attentive. Be culturally involved. You are a Monday through Saturday disciple too. You have a heart for your people, or this message wouldn't matter. Who you are comes from God, and who you reach is of God. Your daily interactions have massive implications if you see them as such with eyes of faith. Show me what you do during the week, and I'll show you your true ministry.

Pay attention to who's present.

Here's what happened at the gate for Stephen: "But he, full of the Holy Spirit, gazed into heaven and saw the glory of God, and Jesus standing at the right hand of God" (Acts 7:55). "Then they cast him out of the city and stoned him. And the witnesses laid down their garments at the feet of a young man named Saul" (v. 58). "And Saul approved of his execution" (8:1).

Stephen had a finite mind like you and me. He couldn't tell from the crowd who would receive what he was saying or not. We know because of Scripture that Saul, a strong hater of Jesus, was there, and quite possibly so was Philip, a friend of Stephen who was also chosen to serve. Their lives were changed because of Stephen. And Jesus was present too.

Jesus is always present. I don't think anyone else saw Jesus that day, but Stephen did. Many people saw Jesus in Stephen, but only Stephen saw Jesus. He gave Stephen a standing ovation. Think about this. I believe it to be the first of many standing ovations. When someone dies for Christ, He stands for them. We will all die, but we will not all be martyred. He welcomes us all, but He stands for those who stand for Him.

Saul was present. The haters will always be around as long as Jesus tarries. Saul hated everything Stephen stood for and loved every effort to bring disciples of Jesus down. Do you have people in your life who don't get your faith or commitment to church or your lifestyle?

How is Stephen's account and the rest of Scripture helpful and relevant today? How are you currently being affected by others who make it their mission to serve one another?

It's because of what Martin Luther King Jr., Mother Teresa, and Mahatma Gandhi did at the gate that we keep telling their stories today. I was paying attention to what my mom was doing at the gate and am now in the company of enthusiastic witnesses. Who were you watching? Who are you watching? Who's watching you? You both might be unaware. We don't know if Stephen and Saul knew each other. They certainly weren't friends, but Saul was present and witnessed Stephen's wisdom and love for Jesus Christ.

Perhaps Philip had every intention of heading down to Samaria to preach Jesus after he finished waiting on tables that day. But then this uproar happened, and a close friend and follower of Jesus was murdered.

I suggest that Philip was a part of it, although his story only picks up when he went to Samaria in Acts 8. He was selected at the same time Stephen was, and after the stoning, Philip went down to Samaria and proclaimed Christ and shared Scripture with the government official from Ethiopia. Today, 62 percent of the Ethiopian population are Christians, and Philip had something to do with this.[1] He shared what he knew with someone who was interested.

While you are paying attention to culture, culture could be paying attention to you. This was Philip's story because of Stephen's stoning. "Philip went down to the city of Samaria and proclaimed to them the Christ. And the crowds with one accord paid attention to what was being said by Philip, when they heard him and saw the [wonders and] signs he did" (8:5–6).

Who seems to be watching your life? Stephen's story caused people to scatter and preach the Word wherever they went. It is recorded in the famous faith chapter that, as disciples gave their lives for Jesus, the world was not worthy of them (Heb. 11:37–38). For the world not to consider us worthy deems us worthy in the eyes of Christ.

We are of the company of enthusiastic witnesses.

"And the word of God continued to increase, and the number of disciples multiplied greatly" (Acts 6:7). "Now those who were scattered went about preaching the word" (8:4).

When we see God do something, that makes us witnesses. The American church talks about statistics, while the Head of the church calls us into stories—stories happening during the week right here at home. (In chapter 18, I'll explain that Sundays are for story swapping and Mondays are for story stepping.)

Kenneth Scott Latourette, an early twentieth-century professor of missions and Oriental history at Yale University, coined the phrase I'm using: the "company of enthusiastic witnesses."[2] Belief in the resurrection

> was the belief that turned heartbroken followers of a crucified rabbi into the courageous witnesses and martyrs of the early church . . . turned them into the community of the resurrection. You could imprison them, flog them, kill them, but you could not make them deny their conviction that "on the third day he rose again." . . . They were made over into a company of enthusiastic witnesses.[3]

When Jesus appeared to the disciples after his resurrection, he said this to them:

> "These are my words that I spoke to you while I was still with you, that everything written about me in the Law of Moses and the Prophets and the Psalms must be fulfilled." Then he opened their minds to understand the Scriptures, and said to them, "Thus it is written, that the Christ should suffer and on the third day rise from the dead, and that repentance for the forgiveness of sins should be proclaimed in his name to all nations, beginning from Jerusalem. You are witnesses of these things. And behold, I am sending the promise of my Father upon you. But stay in the city until you are clothed with power from on high." (Luke 24:44–49)

He opened their minds to understand what the Bible said and pointed out that what they saw personally had been recorded in the Bible. He was connecting their lives to God's Word. He was also telling them to go tell *all* the nations, starting at home—once they were filled with the Holy Spirit. This is the company of enthusiastic witnesses! Disciples of Jesus today can trace our stories back to these first disciples who told others . . . who told still others . . . until someone told us. I traveled to Jerusalem one week prior to the global outbreak of COVID-19. I sat on the Mount of Olives and let the truth pour over me that this was where my spiritual roots began. It is where all our spiritual roots begin.

Stephen had no idea we'd still be talking about his incredible love for God and his people. What happens at the gate doesn't stay at the gate because of who is present and the company we keep. It's the Bible, God's central message, that connects us with culture and Christ.

Practice.

Read your Bible. It just might save someone's life.

7 Connect with Christ and Culture

There is no obligation to go further. You choose to continue or not. I cannot predict for you where God will take you. I can only say if you do continue, adventure will follow and the Holy Spirit will be your companion. In my years on earth, I very much want to wear down the paths between the gate, the cross, and the table with many others because I have found Jesus worth following. Have you?

Our global reality is one of many ways and many paths. A constant echo around the world is that there must be more than one way to God. People are either searching for or have found a way that works for them. Is there just one way?

Jesus said, "I am the way, the truth, and the life! . . . Without me, no one can go to the Father" (John 14:6 CEV). Many people will identify and support Jesus's teachings. You could ask anyone, "Do you ever take care of the sick and hungry? Do you turn the other cheek? Do you put others before yourself? Do you do for others as you would have them do for you?" I find it fascinating that Jesus spoke of the narrow gate immediately after the Golden Rule that most religions and cultures seek to follow. He said, "Enter by the narrow gate. For the gate is wide and the way easy that leads to destruction, and those who enter by it are many. For the gate is narrow and the way is hard that leads to life, and those who find it are few" (Matt. 7:13–14).

Then what are the many doing who haven't entered the narrow gate? Do we talk with them about what comes next? "Can I show you what can save your life? May I introduce you to a life of purpose and meaning? I'd love to lead you through the narrow gate. The way you're doing life is going through the wide gate and taking the easy way." Do we explain how choosing the wide and easy is making your own faith cocktail of sorts? "When you decide you can call the shots, set the boundaries, determine right from wrong, and take a bit from here and there, mixing and matching, you're not following the way of Jesus."

When translating Jesus, the marketplace gate always intersects with the narrow gate. Christ came to connect with culture. God sent His Son Jesus to show you how much He loves you. He chose not to do this from a throne in heaven but to put human flesh on, come and find you right where you are, and put His arms around you and lead you to an abundant, everlasting life. We're not just at the gate to be kind. We're at the gate because the love of Christ compels us to share His love with others. We need to speak with the mindfulness of culture and with the love of Christ. We learn culture by paying attention. We learn Christ through prayer.

I propose a cultural framework for a conversation about Jesus: go narrow. Go through. Then go wide. *Going narrow* is

Christ's plan to set boundaries we can live and thrive in for our good and the good of humanity. *Going through* is our agreement to the invisible reality of one way through Jesus Christ. *Going wide* is encountering freedom on the other side of the narrow gate. As a disciple of Jesus, you recognize this is the decision you made to follow Christ. You entered the narrow gate, believing Jesus is the only way, truth, and life, and you are living on the other side of this redemptive reality. At the same time, you are being given a way to translate this to someone.

Keep in mind that people are unpredictable. That's why we continue translating Jesus. If Jesus Himself came and not everyone was receptive, you can assume not all will receive His love through you. How we speak about Christ matters. Culture does affect how we share Him. This is because of shifts in culture, in thinking. Not because Christ has changed. The Good News of Jesus is the same as it was in 580, 1272, 1731, and this year. Who will go narrow, go through, go wide?

Go narrow.

Why have one way when you can have three ways? Greed is a worldly trait, and perhaps the world with its many options is at fault for making the narrow gate look uninviting. Yet Jesus has always been minimal, direct, and clear. *Enter the narrow gate. I am the way.* Restrictions have a negative connotation for us. How do you act toward boundaries?

In our toddler's discovery of their world, we go to great lengths to keep them protected and safe so they can explore. Plastic guards are inserted in electrical outlets. Breakable decor is put out of reach. A gate is installed on the stairwell. These boundaries are for their good, not their harm. These boundaries are set up in love.

We first look to boundaries to see what we can and cannot do. Then why do we get disgruntled when it comes to who's in control of the universe and our lives? Why do we not want boundaries there? We are a rebellious and fearful people, especially when it comes to what we cannot see. We are all looking for the bumper pads, and when the lines aren't clear, we are prone to build our own beliefs and ways and rules and systems.

Imagine a world where the ocean has no bounds. Imagine a city with no park rules or regulations. Imagine a transportation hub with no requirements for tickets or times. Imagine your work environment with no schedules. It is because of boundaries that you can thrive in life.

When we think of Jesus being the only way, consider that most work cultures have a narrow way. Protocol is in place for doing the job a certain way in your context and work environment. Your work culture has a rule book, style guide, or order of operations that gives order and clarity to the organization. In fact, if you can't execute the vision, your job is on the line—it's that crucial. Or think of a narrow way along the lines of how you decline a sweet treat or carbs at a restaurant: you can do it because you're on a restricted diet or health plan. People say this self-control leads to freedom, not bondage. At first glance, I see how the way of Jesus looks restrictive. I see why people frown to learn that the only way to God is through Jesus. Isn't that too exclusive?

Narrow, yes. But not exclusive. I believe it's a narrow gate because it helps us leave everything else, to set it all down. All of us can enter—one by one—because it's an individual decision. Think turnstiles. A mass of people wait for the park to open, but eventually every individual has to enter the turnstile before getting to run free in the park!

We all want boundaries and for someone to have more control and authority than we ourselves possess. We want to hope the world is being held up and the sun won't get any closer than it is, and people can change and be healed and restored, and that someone can bring peace and end violence once and for all. Can we accept the boundaries Jesus brings?

Go through.

Everyone is making a decision today. Sides are chosen to go through the narrow gate or not. Joseph Loconte parallels J. R. R. Tolkien's and C. S. Lewis's writings in making a decision for following Jesus:

> The choice they face is also a summons; not a blind accident, but a Calling on their lives. One may answer the Call—or refuse it, turn away, and walk into Darkness. But indifference to the Call to struggle against evil is not an option; one must take sides.[1]

At the gate, many believe and are okay with God, like my rideshare driver. It gets harder with Jesus because of His claims of being the only way to God and the only way to salvation. This is the toughest part of sharing our faith; there's no way around Jesus, and it's why He calls it the narrow gate that only a few find. Stott says, "We cannot remain neutral. Nor can we just drift into Christianity. Nor can anyone else settle the matter for us. We must decide for ourselves."[2] Faith in God, though invisible, requires intention and decision. People will find reasons not to believe and follow Jesus. Your testimony might cause them to question their lack of trust in God. Such people will seek you out if how you live proves their reasons lacking.

We can use logic, love, and faith to make this decision to believe the one way to God is through the person of Jesus. To go through the narrow gate is to believe and align with this reality. "One way" has a bad reputation, and many paths get praised. But what if one way was all we needed? By offering us one way, Jesus simplifies life and makes it satisfying.

Is it logic that makes Jesus seem unreasonable? How much reason and logic do you need to know you're loved by your spouse, parent, child, or best friend? What is love? "God sent His only Son [Jesus] into the world, so that we might live through him" (1 John 4:9). In this is love. We didn't do anything and can't do anything to earn it. To declare Jesus is the Son of God and is Love—the definition, founder, origin, continuation, fulfillment, and embodiment—is to declare the truth and purity of love. *Jesus loves me.* This is not animated love, romantic-comedy love, abstract love. Free your mind from these. To go through the narrow gate is to go in love. Jesus loves you. It's a love like no other. He instituted love at creation when He chose to make you, form you, and breathe life in you—into your soul. The core of you is lacking until you fill it with Jesus's love.

In my conversations with non-Christians, I hear them say they feel like they've got to know and grasp and believe 100 percent to be a Christian. It's in all of us to want to present our best selves to an offer like this. But committed disciples of Jesus know every discovery and every day brings new growth and an awareness there's still so much to learn and still so much to understand about being loved by Him.

Around the narrow gate, people are passing each other by with wrong assumptions. "Listen up!" we can say. "Jesus is the way, the truth, and the life. The only way to the Father is through Him. Believe in Him by confessing He is Lord, and choose this day to learn more about Him—at the same time letting Him love you. It may be awkward and vastly different and strange, but let Him love you."

How we relate to God will be different for each of us. He loves us. He wants to journey this life with us. He created us and knows what's best. He wants us to get to know Him more every day. We do this through praying in the Spirit, reading the Scriptures, thinking on the truths already planted in our minds, engaging in Christian community, and developing our spiritual awareness. And it will happen. A relationship, that is. Between each of us and Jesus. It's not a checklist or a kit to put together. It's moments that are so intimate and deep. This relationship has its seasons—new growth, hope, waiting, harvest, and pruning.

Go to the end of your life and work backward. Don't you want the cross to be true here in this one life because you hope it's true for the afterlife?

Go wide.

How does freedom feel? Inexpressible freedom awaits on the other side of our yes to Christ. Receiving Jesus is not receiving all the answers. Receiving Jesus is being free from having all the answers, for He is the answer and we live in Him. The figuring out of faith and giving Jesus our lives happens as we run in the path of His commands, because He has freed us. King David wrote, "I run in the path of your commandments, for you have set my heart free" (Ps. 119:32 WEB). Other translations say, "for you enlarge my heart." It's a narrow gate but not a narrow pasture! German theologian Karl Rahner wrote, "The narrow passes which *you* enter soon open out into broad liberty."[3]

The only way to the cross of salvation is through Jesus, the gate, and it's His disciples who have already found Him worth following who travel between the gate of Christ and the gate of marketplace, adding to the table by way of the cross. This is evangelism. This is discipleship. We enter the kingdom of freedom! This is what you see Christians doing in the world today who are freedom runners, and also what the spiritual giants of the past, whom we look back at and model our lives after, have done.

At the gate, the societal marketplace, Jesus teaches us how to engage with culture, and He personified Himself as the gate, saying, "I am the gate; whoever enters through me will be saved. They will come in and go out, and find pasture" (John 10:9 NIV). Might I suggest that because Jesus is salvation, with this freedom we move about the gate, the cross, and the table because we know who we are in Christ.

It is Jesus. He is the way—everything else that claims to be savior is a lie. Harsh it may seem, but when each goes through, they will see. It's all a step of faith that leads to solid ground. I hope, as our friends spend time with us at the gate, the freedom they see in us will help them see that Jesus being the only way is not restrictive.

On this side of the cross, we think we're living wide with many ways to God, but after we choose Jesus, then come wide pastures to run in freedom. Jesus invites you to be a freedom runner! Paul felt this and wrote to the people of Corinth, "We have spoken freely to you, Corinthians; our heart is wide open" (2 Cor. 6:11). When we speak Christ to culture, we are free and open. We speak what we know. We speak from our personal story. Paul also wrote, to the people of Rome, "But thank God you've started listening to a new master, one whose commands set you free to live openly in *his* freedom. I'm using this freedom language because it's easy to picture" (Rom. 6:18–19 Message).

I want to introduce people to the love of Jesus that is available to them and visible in me, but I've set down the pressure that it's up to me. What is up to me—to us—is to make, baptize, and teach. This is what I'll help you with in the next section. You will start conversations and look for open and closed doors. You will be able to share Jesus unashamedly. This is the good news that we have heard and will tell. Christians have the best news in their possession, and Jesus changes everything for all humankind. When in conversation with someone about Jesus, it will be up to them to respond to this good news.

Practice.

Let Him love you. Really let Him love you.

THE CROSS

IF YOU LOVE ME, KEEP MY COMMANDS.

John 14:15 NIV

One day I received a text from Monty's mom:

> Monty's found Jesus and I don't know what to do.
> Will you meet with him?

It disrupted my entire day. And truthfully, I haven't and hopefully never will recover from this disruption.

As his mom reached out to me, Monty himself submitted something similar to our church online. They had been watching services. They were clicking around the website, and he found the baptism video and decided that seemed to be his next step. But his mom had a different next step.

Monty was our son's classmate and soccer teammate, but Ben and I hadn't seen him in over three years, and for a teenager, so much changes in that amount of time. When he found us in the back of the coffee shop, he seemed so handsome and tall to us. He actually looked like he'd met Jesus! Monty told us about a friend who'd introduced him to Jesus in the chat room while school was online during the pandemic. He shared how he'd prayed to follow Jesus and waited a few days to be filled with the Holy Spirit. This sharp-looking young man glowed as he gleefully described a "lovey-dovey feeling that felt like a warm flame."

I didn't know what was happening. I was looking into this young man's eyes and suddenly it felt like he was deeply connected to us as we all experienced this supernatural exchange over coffee and milkshakes. Though all three of us had found our way to the cross from different backgrounds and experiences, I never doubted his story. The marks of authenticity were as clear as the smile on his face. He showed us his old music playlist and his current playlist. He spoke about being sick to his stomach toward the habits that had been present just weeks prior.

"Every year you and Elijah were in elementary school together, your name was on his bedroom wall," we told him. "We prayed regularly for you, Monty." Our prayers weren't for his salvation, necessarily. They were for friendship and sick days and kickball wins.[4]

We were all undone. When you get a glimpse of how much Jesus loves you, you can't help but love Him back.

8 Learn the Language

Water is ancient. The water you drank today could have been the parted water of the Red Sea or a fraction from the flood in Noah's day.[1] Water, always being recycled and reclaimed, is the most fluid commodity on Planet Earth as it runs through the hydrologic cycle, evaporating as gas, coming down as liquid, and, when the temperature is just right, becoming a solid.

The language of Christ is fluid like water. It comes in and out in various forms. We breathe in His Spirit as we take in His written and spoken Word, and we exhale His Spirit as we intercede for others and share His truths. Just as without water we die, without the language of Christ, which is prayer, we perish.

This language we use is both ancient and always new. When we pray, we communicate with Christ and experience Him. We can talk with one another or with ourselves about peace and hope and healing and what God has done in the past. Not until we pray do we use language to communicate directly to Him.

We translate Jesus to others as we first spend time with Him. Notice the language in three forms—prayer, Scripture, and the Holy Spirit—in these examples:

- We read about His forgiveness in *Scripture*. We *pray* for His forgiveness. We personally experience His forgiveness that empowers us to forgive others by the *Holy Spirit*.
- We bring our cares and worries to God in *prayer*. We believe His *scriptural* promise in Philippians 4:6–7 that His peace will guard our hearts and minds. People will be able to see this peace in us, for it's a fruit of the *Holy Spirit's* activity in our lives.
- We *pray* for our friends and family to know the love of Jesus. *Scripture* teaches us to share what we know about Him. The *Holy Spirit* gives us the words to say (Luke 12:12).

Do you see how each aspect of life is found in three language forms of Christ? In this chapter, I want to show you multiple ways we learn how to speak Christ. We do this in a culture that consults Google, humanity's instinctive first search. We Google our symptoms before we make a doctor's appointment. We Google directions before we drive. We Google prayer before we even consider giving prayer a try. My friend, Google is limited. Let's go to the unlimited source. Oh, that the language of Christ will be sacred to us again! To listen and learn from Christ by spending time with Him—this is the greatest use of our time.

Father, teach us to pray. Let Your Word dwell in us. Come, Holy Spirit.

Teach us to pray.

Maybe you're thinking, *I can't pray. I don't know how to pray. Prayer is too hard. I've tried and given up because I couldn't connect or He didn't answer.*

In the name of Jesus in this present moment, I pray against prayerlessness for you and me.

Father God, teach us to pray like You taught Your disciples to pray (Luke 11:1).

My friend says, "I don't know how to pray or the words to use or where to start." My discomforting reply is "I don't either." But we start to pray anyway. We say His name—Jesus—and thus a prayer has begun!

Prayer is being with God. It's as real as we are in the invisible presence of almighty God. In prayer, we experience what can't be held or touched but what cherishes and changes us. The Bible tells us Jesus prayed like this:

> In the days of his flesh, Jesus offered up prayers and supplications, with loud cries and tears, to him who was able to save him from death, and he was heard because of his reverence. (Heb. 5:7)

Let us then mindfully enter into prayer.

Enter with mystery. Our God defies logic and time and space. What we bring before Him, both the trivial and challenging, isn't for us to fully grasp but to fully entrust to His good and capable hands.

God, You are great and "in your hand it is to make great and to give strength to all" (1 Chron. 29:12).

Enter with gratitude. Recognize who Jesus is and what He has done for us. Make sure to include today, always!

God, this is the day You have made. I will "rejoice and be glad in it" (Ps. 118:24).

Enter with partnership. He delights that we come to Him with anything and everything and will show us in prayer what to do. We have a better possibility of knowing what to do because of prayer than without it.

God, I do not know what to do, but "[my] eyes are on you" (2 Chron. 20:12).

Prayer is being quiet and letting God speak to us. To hear Him, we need to turn all the other voices off. That can take a minute, but you'll seemingly gain those minutes back when it's just you and Him. Imagine all the lights being on in your home and, in order to go to bed, you need to turn them all off. Preparing to pray is like that: going through your mental thoughts and turning them off so all you've got left is space to hear from God.

We best grasp prayer when we're open to always growing in this spiritual discipline. We are continually facing new situations where we get to practice prayer. Prayer is not restricted to a place or occasion. I can pray on the bus and in the dental chair. I can pray at the kitchen sink and backstage. I can talk to God before I talk to a client, and I can close my eyes and listen to His voice in the stillness of the night.

Christ put a spin on this language of prayer in His first public sermon: "But I say to you, Love your enemies [at the gate] and pray for those who persecute you [at the cross]" (Matt. 5:44). Making a conscious effort to love someone by your actions is translating Jesus. By definition, an enemy's intentions are to make life difficult for you. Your response to love will not be lost on them. You translate Jesus, bringing Him to light when you turn the other cheek, let your enemy have your cloak, go with them two miles, and give graciously to them (vv. 38–44). Prayer is a language that, when we use it, gets us closer to God and able to see things happen.

Let the Word dwell in you.

If the Bible has become just another book on the shelf or in your study, may you pick it up and kiss it. Kiss it and hold it tight. Give it extra attention on behalf of our brothers and sisters who have been robbed of this precious, tangible book that still is alive and active.

> Let the word of Christ dwell in you richly, teaching and admonishing one another in all wisdom, singing psalms and hymns and spiritual songs, with thankfulness in your hearts to God. And whatever you do, in word or deed, do everything in the name of the Lord Jesus, giving thanks to God the Father through him. (Col. 3:16–17)

Because God made us and knows what we need, He continually speaks through His Word to address and comfort us with His love. His Word is always for our good, our correction, and our discipline (2 Tim. 3:16).

We know when Scripture occupies space in us, we are affected by its residence. In his book *Basic Christianity*, John Stott writes,

> The Bible will not allow us to retreat from these practical responsibilities into mystical seclusion or into a so-called Christian fellowship that tries to insulate itself from the world. . . . It is comparatively simple to ease this tension by withdrawing into Christ and neglecting the world, or by so involving ourselves in the world as to forget Christ. . . . The balanced Christian who

takes the Bible as their guide will seek to live equally and simultaneously "in Christ" and "in the world." We cannot opt out of either.[2]

Preach, John! I have found God's written Word:

Motivates me to action.

Prompts me to a conversation.

Inserts a pause in my decision-making.

Recenters the wandering eyes of my heart.

Initiates the call in me to forgive.

Gets in me and runs through my veins. (I don't know how this happens.)

Makes me feel things for others. (I can't explain this either.)

Have you experienced something like this when you've read His Word?

The beauty of the people of the cross is that we cling to His Word, one book, that teaches us all. We're not grabbing at just anything. The Bible is intellectually stimulating, historical and artistic, practical and persuasive, and still the bestselling book of all time. "We must learn to read the Bible in company," encourages Alister McGrath.[3] Without consistent time in God's Word, we cannot claim to be disciples—learners of Jesus.

Receive the Holy Spirit.

The Trinity is the whole picture. Our Creator God gives us our landscape, our footing, our surroundings, our tangible reality. Living among us as the Son of God, Jesus gives us a perfect example of how to love God and love others. Now the Holy Spirit lives inside His disciples and gives us the supernatural ability to communicate with each other in the Spirit as He works through our physical bodies.

The Holy Spirit was just as fear-inducing to me as the devil for most of my life. I didn't know enough about Him and hadn't heard enough stories about His activity to know I would want to like Him. I knew He was on the good side, but that was about it. Then I began to hear stories of the Holy Spirit's activity, but it was long before I saw a meeting place shaken and filled with the Holy Spirit.

One day, I was praying together with a group of friends in a living room, and we witnessed the Holy Spirit upon us. I didn't have a framework or an explanation for what was happening other than *This is not of us*. It wasn't something we conjured up. The writers of the New Testament did a good job explaining what took place two thousand years ago, but after you've experienced God at work, you kind of get that it's not that easy to describe.

I'm certain that is God's point—to do things in our midst that can't be fully explained. Have you experienced God at work in a way that defies logic and reason and explanation? We don't have the power to reproduce any of His actions; what we do have is access to the same Holy Spirit, who can be invited and unleashed into any environment where faith is present.

Just before Christ died, He promised His disciples they would receive another Helper/Advocate/Counselor to be with them and in them forever (John 14:16–17). It was in a private room with locked doors that Jesus just appeared in His resurrected body and commissioned the disciples to live *sent*. "And when he had said this, he breathed on them and said to them, 'Receive the Holy Spirit'" (20:22).

Salvation happens once, yet we spend our lifetimes experiencing the ongoing rescue from ourselves and our sins through the restorative work of the Holy Spirit. The Holy Spirit is a person who changes us when we accept Him and welcome Him into our lives. He takes up residence in us and develops Christlike characteristics in us—fruit of the Spirit, as Paul called them. Jesus was baptized in the Spirit; so you also are to be baptized in the Spirit, disciple. Jesus was led by the Spirit; so are you, His follower, to be led by the Spirit. Jesus was filled with the Spirit; so are His disciples to be filled with the Spirit.

We call on the Spirit of the living God in prayer as we open the Scriptures and at any moment of any day.

Spirit, speak, for I am listening. Spirit, help me understand what I am reading. Spirit, change me to reflect my Savior.

An ancient prayer is *Come, Holy Spirit*. It is as basic as it sounds. Hippolytus, an early church theologian, wrote a prayer for Christians to welcome the Holy Spirit: "And we pray that you will send your Holy Spirit." A thousand years later, the "Come, Holy Spirit" prayer was written as a Latin worship poem called "*Veni Sancte Spiritus*" that became central in Western church worship. In 1980, Californian pastor John Wimber prayed this simple yet profound prayer, "Come, Holy Spirit," among his congregation, and a movement began of inviting the Spirit into their worship gatherings and prayer circles and daily lives. The Vineyard Church in Anaheim began to experience the Spirit's power, healing, and manifestations because of the presence of the living God in their midst.[4] Wimber was invited to speak at

Holy Trinity Brompton Church in London, England, where a dependency upon the Spirit was growing. The Holy Spirit spoke through Wimber and affected HTB's leadership and the growth of the Alpha Course.

In 2019, I volunteered to teach the Alpha Course to a group of seekers in my church in San Francisco. For the first time, I prayed this ancient prayer out loud, with my hands open, not out of mystical hoopla but out of a desire to know Jesus more through the Spirit who lives in me. Since I began praying this prayer on a regular basis, I have better followed the convictions of my heart, stepped out in faith to talk to strangers, and been unified in prayer with other believers around the world who also pray this expectant prayer.

This is why I love writing about the Holy Spirit. He knows I'm writing about Him, and I sense Him writing through my fingers. The Spirit gave John Wimber these words:

> At Babel, one language changed to many, throwing everyone into confusion—resulting in a loss of power and purpose. At Pentecost, many nations and tongues were unified—and those present were able to experience an outpouring of power, and 3,000 new disciples were added.[5]

Father, Son, and Holy Spirit, I pray for three thousand new disciples to come through the reader holding this book.

Prompting.

In the same conversation Jesus had with His disciples during which they asked Him how to pray, He also taught them how to receive the Holy Spirit: "How much more will your Father in heaven give the Holy Spirit to those who ask him!" (Luke 11:13 NIV).

Open your hands. Pray, "Come, Holy Spirit." Then wait on Him to come. He will.

Know the Landscape

When I return to the best little island in the world every summer, I take on a different identity the moment our vehicle turns onto the causeway. I don't live here. I haven't been around for months. I only know a handful of residents. But when I arrive, something happens inside me as I breathe in the salty warm air. I identify as a local for a mere seven days. I shop, bike, walk, unwind. I bask in the evening sunsets on the intercoastal waterway and wake to meet the same sun on the Atlantic side hours later. The only times I think of San Francisco are when the thought enters my mind, *All my friends need to visit this place!* I become one with the island and her people. When I see tourists with a map, I am determined to help them embrace the island as I have. Every time our family returns, some of us set out to find discoveries we've read or heard about but haven't yet found ourselves.

For one week I'm consumed with island life. I take it upon myself to connect deeply and with more meaning. If a new local book has been written, I grab it from the bookstore. If a new restaurant has opened, I'll give it a try despite reviews. I love this place. I tell myself that when I have to leave, I'll take its relaxing vibes and chill demeanor home with me—and for a few days, this works. But not until I return to the island again can I truly take on its mentality and charm and way of living. Maybe you have a place like this too.

We go to the cross because it's where Jesus came down to us. The point of the cross is to be *the* point—not a onetime experience but a frequent prayer, place, purpose, position, power, and presence. Followers of Jesus don't chart their own path. They grow to delight in the well-worn path.

You've come to the cross once to say you believe Jesus is the Son of God and to receive forgiveness for your sins. What keeps you from returning? It's probably the very reason our nonbelieving friends don't want to go either. Isaiah says all we've done is meaningless, detestable, worthless, and burdensome to God. What are we to do then? I love how God says, "Let's settle this." There is a way, and it's to the cross.

> "Come now, let us settle the matter," says the LORD.
> "Though your sins are like scarlet,
>   they shall be as white as snow;
> though they are red as crimson,
>   they shall be like wool." (Isa. 1:18 NIV)

Jesus beckons us to come again. To let Him love us.

How do we love Jesus back? We die for Him as He died for us. There is Jesus and me, then there is Jesus in me. This happens when "I have been crucified with Christ. It is no longer I who live, but Christ who lives in me" (Gal. 2:20). Jesus on the cross looks at us with love. Jesus in His dying did so in love.

The same happens as we die to our old self, our own path. His love fills us. We are one with Him. In an odd and mysterious way, it's Christ's love that makes it possible for us to love Christ in return.

The cross is for both coming and going.

The Christian faith is rarely linear. We are called to be the persistent widow before the judge. To pray without ceasing. To keep knocking, seeking, asking. To come in and out of the gate, meeting people in the marketplace and introducing them to Jesus. To gather people around the table, start a conversation, and pick it back up next time. The way of Jesus takes us back to the cross to remember, to die to ourselves, to reckon with His humanity and divinity, to meet others. Repentance also brings us back to the cross again and again and again. We will be passing one another as we practice the languages of culture and Christ at the gate, the cross, and the table.

Repentant people are receptive people. Non-Christians need to see Christians going on an ongoing basis to and from the cross on which our Savior bled and died and suffered for all of us. We go for ourselves, certainly, but we also go on behalf of our friends who have yet to believe. It will not be the church that saves them but always and forever it will be the cross of Jesus Christ that bids them come.

Tiffany has helped me see this more clearly. In her exploration of Christianity, she sees humankind with souls that will be filled with something. It's not visible like our physical beings, yet these interior workings control what our physical beings do. Our flesh that is totally us is prone to living apart from Christ and in the hands of the enemy. Scripture says those who are in Christ are new creations. We have the mind of Christ. We can take captive every thought and align it with truth.[1]

I told Tiffany I'm learning to name and journal my sin struggles. This has been a healthy practice. I write down everything from how I speak to my kids, to how I fight for control over small things, to how I obsess over tasks, to judgmental and covetous thoughts of others. These are all destructive to the abundant life I want in Christ.

Tiffany responded that it makes sense to bring our sins to light and then work intentionally to squash them. When she thinks about how sin has affected her relationship with God, she's noticed that most times sin leads her to push God away. She feels ashamed and unworthy of His love, then embarrassed to face Him.

"It's a vicious cycle," Tiffany shared with me. "It's the main reason I waited awhile to become a Christian. Up until the day I marked the moment with you, Shauna, I always felt a tug on my heart. It showed up big, especially during worship. More and more, I found myself breaking down into tears at certain lyrics. It was a desperation and yearning to be close to God, but I didn't let my walls down because I never felt ready or perfect enough for Him. Looking back, that was a dark period. I don't think I came to that realization until after I put my faith in Jesus."

"Tiffany, there is only so far any of us can go on our own," I said.

"I know I still have the tendency to push Him away when I've sinned and feel ashamed," she said. "So this is something I want to be more aware of, and I want to be more intentional about coming back to God again and again."

Don't you love her honesty? What I see in Tiffany is the landscape of the cross. It's ripe with repentance but also with the fear of not being perfect already.

Let's normalize repentance. Jesus tells us it's a regular practice for His people. It's just human sorrow to say, "Oh, I shouldn't have done that." Every human being can feel this. For Christians, this is the moment of Holy Spirit conviction that leads us to repentance. Non-Christians don't have the Spirit getting their attention for the Father, but we all feel the gap between what we want to be and what we are sometimes. We first come to our senses, like the prodigal son, then return to our Father for His love, grace, forgiveness, and restoration.

To *repent* means to change our minds and go the other way. Our disappointments, frustrations, and questions are not meant to keep us away from the cross but to bring us to Jesus because He loves us. Love brings freedom. Jesus is love and brings freedom not in fractions but in full. When we normalize repentance, there is nothing we won't return to God for.

This doesn't mean we understand it all or can see clearly the path back to God, but it's a decision we make to consciously turn back to God and His ways. As Christians, we are to practice repentance and also teach repentance. To teach there is another direction to go. To teach life is not meant to be this way, with self-reliance, workaholism, shame, being driven by guilt, isolation, dependence on unhealthy relationships, and barely surviving parenting and paychecks.

Tiffany and I meet at the cross, personally and communally. We pass each other often. We share in His sufferings.

The cross is for both suffering and sharing.

The cross isn't pretty. Society wants a way around it in order to avoid conflict and crucifixion. Better, instead, to look for a unicorn to lead us down a cheerful, lighthearted path. But followers of Jesus who find Him ravishing refuse to water Him down. Rather, we offer a simple yet incomplete explanation of suffering, such as these words from Nicky Gumbel:

> Suffering is not part of God's original created order (Gen. 1–2). There was no suffering in the world before rebellion against God. There will be no suffering when God creates a new heaven and a new earth (Rev. 21:3–4). Suffering is, therefore, an alien intrusion into God's world.
>
> So much suffering is caused by us choosing not to love God or others. "The sorrows of those will increase who run after other gods" (Ps. 16:4).[2]

Christians translate Jesus when we share in *His* suffering and with others in their suffering.

Not all will want to stay around the cross of Christ—including us. Suffering is included, and I make no apologies. We don't always expect it and act shocked when it happens, but it's there to unite us with our Savior.

You've consciously chosen to look upon Christ's act of love and make another decision. *Will I join with Christ and die also to my sins that had Him here in the first place?*

Oswald Chambers insists we are to attend our own funeral if we are to be found alive in Christ.[3] The cross is death. No way around it. Death is necessary to be a Christian. "If anyone would come after me, let him deny himself and take up his cross and follow me" (Matt. 16:24). To know the landscape is to know the cross again and again. You cannot be a Christian without suffering for Christ. He taught His disciples that He must suffer many things. He spoke plainly about this. To not receive this truth is to not have in mind the things of God but the things of humankind (Mark 8:31–34). To suffer is to leave a life of self-focus, self-ambition, and self-obsession to be Jesus-focused, Jesus-ambitious, and Jesus-obsessed.

And it is only because we are now Jesus-focused that we can bear to share in the suffering of others. We experience compassion and mercy as Christians and simultaneously feel heavyhearted for our world generally and for our friends specifically. Galatians 6:2 says we are to bear one another's burdens and, when we do, we honor Jesus.

Have you ever felt heavyhearted for someone because of conflict, injustice, or persecution? What did you do about it? Did you repeatedly brush it off and numb your heart from experiencing the emotional roller coaster on their behalf? *This isn't my battle. It's not my fault. They got themselves into this. I'll give them money if they'll just leave me alone.*

I'll be at the cross again, for in these responses I must repent.

As we suffer in this way, we say to God in prayer, "God, I feel this burden. My heart is heavy; come and carry this with me. I cast it on You, for You care for me and them. This was the point of the cross: for You to bear our sins and our shame and to suffer for all of us." Only the cross makes the transaction possible.

In raising our four children, I recall a season when two of them were experiencing hard things in their teenage years. Ben and I carried their burdens. They were suffering and, as I look back, I can see they were dying to self and becoming more like

Christ. Ben and I watched as they wrestled in their faith. *Does God care? Does it matter if I believe in Him? Does He see me? Do I need Him?* We prayed with them often. We interceded and felt compassion for them. We cast our collective burdens on the Lord and counted on the promise that He cares for us. This suffering was worth it. We all got more of Christ and died to our in-the-way flesh in the process. We grew a deeper love for one another, for that's a side effect of being burden bearers.

If you were told you could get all or half of your best friend, what would you take? All or half of your talents? All or half of Jesus? We must share in His sufferings. I will suffer with Christ if it means I know Him more by dying to self and bearing one another's burdens. This also translates Jesus to those who are suffering.

We look upon the cross and immediately think *death*. We shrug it off or walk away, as if by doing so we will avoid death and suffering. No, my friend. It will come to us all. The cross bids you come and die now to be resurrected with Him now, rather than die without Him and without His resurrection. Missionary Sadhu Sundar Singh grew up a Sikh and encountered Jesus in a dream shortly after his mother's death. His experience compelled him to write, "If we do not bear the cross of the Master, we will have to bear the cross of the world, with all its earthly goods. Which cross have you taken up? Pause and consider."[4]

The cross is for both the culture and the church.

With Jesus it's both/and. We can have friends whom society loves and those it rejects. We can engage in meaningful conversations with Christians and skeptics. We can be at dinners with people from different political parties and points of view. We can serve our rich and poor neighbors. Yes, Scripture says to be in the world but not of the world, but the church has plunged deep in both extreme directions.

Crucified and risen Lord, lead us back to our salvation sto-ries and remind us we were strangers to You so we can go be friends to strangers.

So where does the church fit into translating Jesus at the cross? The church is what culture sees when they picture Jesus. The cross is what Christians see when they picture Jesus. The truth is, we'd love for culture to see the church looking at Jesus and therefore see Jesus too—or at least ask us to whom we are giving our attention and affection. Jesus's death on the cross would be in vain if it were just an act of love for the righteous people who thought they were following all the commandments and checking all the boxes. The best news we can give society is that the cross is for us all. Jesus beat death and sin, guilt and shame for all of humanity—no exceptions.

Yet church people confuse culture when we try to fit into culture during the week and then try to fit into church on Sundays because we don't know how to be ourselves seven days a week. Culture will see people in the church mess up, and when they do, they need to see us practicing repentance, forgiveness, reconciliation, and restoration.

Christians being at the cross regularly makes it more approachable for our non-Christian friends too. Christians telling their stories of why they go and what happens at the cross makes it more appealing as well. Collectively this is what the church is all about. The church is a people learning the ways of Jesus and practicing the ways of Jesus with one another.

Jesus got our attention on the cross, and we are forever changed. I suggest that once you encounter Jesus on the cross, you will not choose to do life on your own but with other disciples on a regular basis; as the Scriptures say, we are not to neglect meeting together (Heb. 10:25).

With Jesus, there is always good news! I don't have to know much about your church for you to tell me much about your Jesus. Let not the church be your excuse for not talking about your Christ. The point of outreach is not to grow your church but to introduce people to Jesus. The church needs to be all over the place, just like Jesus! He finished His task at the cross and walked out of the borrowed tomb. I hear Him speak to us: *I'm going. Do you want to come with Me?* Walk the well-worn path to the cross and discover we are disciples in and out of church, in and out of the gate, and all around the table.

Prompting.

Go back to the cross, not because Jesus is still on it but because it's where He changes your life.

10 Meet the People

Meth addict? Here.

Police officer? Here.

Prisoner? Here.

Church lady? Here.

Thief? Here.

Abortion doctor? Here.

Anorexic? Here.

Youth leader? Here.

Priest? Here.

Porn addict? Here.

Corrupt government leader? Here.

Single father of two? Here.

You?

I'm here, but I'm also unsure. I feel like I know less about myself when I consider the cross. I feel at a loss because I just had my plans and thoughts under my control—until I looked at

Jesus. Everyone comes to the cross differently, yet Christ did one act of love. Our getting here doesn't define us. What takes place here does. Yes, we love people, but take a minute and look back over the list above. How do you feel about all of them being here too?

Jesus doesn't see us the way we think He sees us. Similarly, Jesus doesn't see others the way we always see them. Do you wonder if you're in the right place when you see who else is here? We cannot judge. Jesus did not leave that up to us when He died for all humanity.

Jesus is for the one who was born in your country and the one who was not. Jesus is for the one who encountered the cross for the first time today and the one who's back for the third time today. Jesus is for the one whom you cannot believe there's space for at the cross and for the one you pray will one day find space at the cross. If any of us are uncomfortable because of who else is here, we are oblivious to the cross.

In learning the language of Christ, we share the space at the cross. Entitlement dies on the well-worn path to get here. Fellow Christians sharpen these language skills in ourselves as we pray and read the Scriptures, and as we experience the presence of God in company. But so do the others at the cross, the ones on that list. At the cross, Jesus Christ reigns over the kingdom of God as King even as He suffers. It's both/and again. It's kingdom and cross. "A king who dies on the cross must be the king of a rather strange kingdom," wrote Dietrich Bonhoeffer.[1] This theologian and hero to my faith suffered in a Nazi prison because of his allegiance to the cross of Christ and was hanged at age thirty-nine. He taught that our speech reflects this strange kingdom and our King who died for us all. We will only speak to others at the cross when we realize that it was a far stretch for Jesus to even speak to us and call us by name.

Who is at the cross? Why are they here? How do we come close to one another?

The curious.

The curious are seekers. This is my friend Lee. She is open— open to religion, to exploring, to knowing her purpose, to finding the truth, to hard discoveries. The curious have open minds and softened spots in their hearts. Curious people might not believe in Jesus yet or think He would come near to them. Our friends can be both looking for Jesus and still not believing.

Curious people do strange things while looking for Jesus. It's in these inexplicable actions of humanity—drunkenness, substance abuse, promiscuity, bingeing on social media and streaming TV, obsessions with fear and fashion and food and fortunes—that we see the longing for something to fill us. But what is strange to us isn't strange to Jesus. Jesus said of Himself, "For the Son of Man came to seek and to save the lost" (Luke 19:10). Nothing scares Jesus. There's nothing He hasn't seen before. The stories are true that He cast out demons, called fishermen, talked to dead people, brought the dead back to life, and let children climb all over Him.

Curious people ask questions. They search the internet for spiritual answers. Curious people come to church. Curious people, like Zacchaeus, climb trees. They get to a place where they can figure things out and learn. And as a result, curious people who find Jesus always get more than they thought they would. That's the Jesus way. He exceeds our expectations.

I have chosen to unlearn some of my evangelism insights over the years as I engage more with the curious and the admirers. It is my friend Lee, who grew up without religion, who teaches me how to be curious and nonjudgmental. She shows me how she loves her adopted son, who is a Christian, and how she honors and respects him.

It is the curious who help us get closer to Christ. Being with others who are starting from scratch or unlearning their childhood religions gives us a variety of lenses through which to see Jesus better. Through conversation about faith, we can see what He is doing in their lives that is different from what He is doing in ours. It's an extraordinary way to love one another. Let us see Christ in the others here at the cross. Love Christ in the other. Listen for Christ in the other. You will find Christ in those who have not found Him in them yet.

As you learn the language of Christ, prayers of intercession work beautifully among curious people. *Jesus, I'm so glad she's here. I know the cross is hard to look upon, but may she see You endured it for her sake and want to love You in return.* I have found the curious welcome prayer. Ask respectfully if you can pray for them. Because they are open, your prayers invite the Holy Spirit to release His love and to reveal Himself to them.

The admirers.

Nineteenth-century Christian philosopher Søren Kierkegaard pointed the admirers out to me. People who keep themselves personally detached are admirers, wrote Kierkegaard.[2] I would add that admirers are personally detached yet present at the most interesting times. It's the admirers who take their posts at the gate entrances and positions along the path of the cross. They have questions. "Who put you in charge? Who elected you gatekeeper?" We know such people. Perhaps we are such people. In our hearts, if not also with our actions, we determine in our personal value system who has access to the cross and who doesn't. We wonder, *Why are they even here at the cross?*

The admirers are the brought-up Christians who think they are good and grandfathered in. They've been exposed to Christianity through religious education, Christian parents, Bible Belt culture. The brought-up Christians know all kinds of things about the Bible and the church and Jesus. Their knowledge makes them feel entitled to the benefits of Christ.

Admirers have secondhand experiences. They show it in their likes and thumbs-up. Admirers feel comfortable when there is a crowd. Their insecurities go away as they cheer with what feels like a majority. But then again, admirers are their own gatekeepers, so they tend to only let like-minded people in and have formed their own party where Jesus wouldn't even get in with His group of friends.

Admirers don't know they are lost and blind, or they have forgotten how their stories began. They have not become followers because they are still picking and choosing. They are the rich young rulers and the rich middle-aged lawyers. They are Judas and Nicodemus, as Kierkegaard suggested. Admirers feel entitled to the name *Christian* and privileged to set political and religious agendas that are in their favor, always and of course.

Do pandemics and media megaphones blow things out of proportion, or do they reveal where our allegiance lies and whom or what we really hold as our king and savior?

The admirer is the greatest fool, loving what cannot be kept and losing precious time on earth. Admirers see their lives and then Jesus. Surrender has been considered by them and classified as unnecessary. How do followers connect with admirers?

Followers act with compassion to others at the cross. They say, "I am glad I am still loved and accepted by a Savior who set me free and forgives me for my ugly thoughts, private habits, secret living, embarrassing motives, and judgmental gazes. And if there's room for me here, then there's certainly room for everyone else too."

Romans 16:17–18 is a word to followers:

> One final word of counsel, friends. Keep a sharp eye out for those who take bits and pieces of the teaching that you learned and then use them to make trouble. Give these people a wide berth. They have no intention of living for our Master Christ. They're only in this for what they can get out of it, and aren't above using pious sweet talk to dupe unsuspecting innocents. (Message)

Jesus, their eyes are open only to the perks of Christianity. Shift their gaze to the Person of Christianity. And if they happen to see me, may I outdo them with Your love and grace and goodness. Make more admirers into Your followers today, I pray.

Scripture speaks to admirers because of their exposure to the faith. However, they also find it offensive when it doesn't seem to benefit them. Kenneth Scott Latourette, a distinguished professor at Yale Divinity School in the early twentieth century, concluded, "It must be obvious to any thoughtful reader of the Gospel records that Jesus regarded himself and his message as inseparable."[3] To follow Jesus is to follow Scripture. To read Scripture is to open yourself up to the Spirit. To open yourself up to the Spirit is to begin a prayer. Share how reading your Bible is impacting your life. Elevate His Word to them. Jesus and Scripture are inseparable. He is both God and man. Both the Word in Spirit and in flesh.

Kierkegaard confronts us again: "What dreadful untruth it is to admire the truth instead of following it."[4]

The follower.

When Jesus said "Follow Me," it's because He's going places. Are you going places with your faith? Or has faith become something you collect? Followers and disciples are called *Christians* because they are the ones who model Christ and take the gospel to people who don't know and haven't heard. It was in Antioch, capital of ancient Syria and leading city of the Roman East, where disciples were first called Christians when they took the Good News of Jesus to the Greeks (Acts 11:26).

Jad had nothing left but money to buy his flight home. Then a spam call came and, unlike usual, he answered it. The caller offered him a job. He could stay! But where had this opportunity come from? Jad began to search. He reached out to a trusted friend—someone who was religious but of a different religion than Jad had known from childhood. This friend made a few suggestions. Jad was willing. He was curious. He had to find answers to who was watching out for him. The search led him to our church. Without any background or knowledge of the language of Christ, he was hesitant to return, but Jad's friend suggested he give it another try. He returned and also signed up for the Alpha Course to better understand the claims of Christ. On his search for someone, Jesus Christ was answering all his questions. Jad became convinced Jesus was real and who He claimed to be! Jesus had been the One all along.

Jesus loved Jad. Jad chose to love Him back by obeying Him. Identifying with Christ would be costly, but he joyfully wanted to be baptized. On a Monday afternoon, with only a handful of people in the room, Jad was buried with Christ and raised with Christ, and he is filled with a pure love for Jesus. I watched as he came up out of the waters and Jesus began to fill him. Jad held his face in his hands, and the Spirit started from the toes up until he was consumed. I've never seen anything like it. Jesus transformed Jad and, through his story, Jesus was translated more clearly to me.

"Follow Me." How can we misinterpret that? Jesus doesn't say "Figure Me out," "Be My admirer," "Join My fan club," or "You've got options here." While Jesus walked the earth, His crowd of admirers dwindled over time. They were there for the healing and miracles, as long as they weren't inconvenienced. Compare the townspeople in Mark 5 to those around when Jesus went on trial in chapter 14. Every person took a side: curious, admirer, or follower. Sides are still taken today.

Followers are not wishy-washy. Christ's disciples have a growth mindset and are graciously learning, but one thing is certain: Jesus is Lord. We have decided to follow Jesus. No turning back.

What makes a follower of Jesus? It's not just what you look back at to mark the moment but also where you are with Christ today. To be a Christ follower is to believe and obey. To trust and obey. From knowledge to action. From head to toe. A supernatural reverence and awe comes upon followers because they *know* who they are and who Jesus is, and that overwhelming and incomprehensible reality compels them to follow Him.

When you're with a follower, you leave refreshed. You see they live for something greater than themselves. They see you because they've seen Jesus. They hear you because they've heard from Jesus. They love you because they know Jesus loves them. I'd rather give people a glimpse of Jesus's love by way of introduction than be compelled to lead with legalism or to first ask them to deal with their way of living before I can bring up Jesus.

Take notice of this interaction between admirers and a new follower. As the tensions rose and the division lines became clearer, the now-seeing man who'd washed in the "pool of Siloam (which means Sent)" (John 9:7) gave his story yet again to the religious people.

"I have told you already and you did not listen. . . . Do you want to become his disciples too?" (v. 27 NIV).

I find it interesting that *disciple* was a divisive word.

"Then they hurled insults at him and said, 'You are this fellow's disciple!'" (v. 28 NIV).

And his response is classic. The once-blind, now-seeing Christ follower answered, "Now that is remarkable!" (v. 30 NIV).

Followers in the first century or today's century can find camaraderie with Thomas à Kempis, a German Christ follower in the 1400s, who penned this:

> There will always be many who love Christ's heavenly kingdom, but few who will bear his cross. . . . He finds many to share his table, but few who will join him in fasting. Many are eager to be happy with him; few wish to suffer anything for him. . . . Many are

awed by his miracles; few accept the shame of his cross. Many love Christ as long as they encounter no hardship; many praise and bless him as long as they receive some comfort from him. But if Jesus hides himself and leaves them for a while, they either start complaining or become dejected. Those, on the contrary, who love him for his own sake and not for any comfort of their own, praise him both in trial and anguish of heart as well as in the bliss of consolation. Even if Jesus should never comfort them, they would continue to praise and thank him. What power there is in a pure love for Jesus—love that is free from all self-interest and self-love![5]

The more you look at followers, the clearer it is who the admirers are. Admirers are all about law, religion, and tradition, but what about the language? People who only speak the language of Christ and refuse to practice the language of culture live with the false certainty they got it all when Christ came into their hearts. They consider the ones who speak culture too worldly and are sure it's ruining their witness.

To the curious, the worst turnoff is to act like you've arrived. You and I haven't. Clearly. We're still on Planet Earth—breathing flesh, vulnerable to sin. The best you can offer to those who don't believe yet is encouragement from your story. How you're on a journey, what you're learning today, and how your life is deeper, richer, fuller than a year or month ago. The curious will follow if they see followers curious still.

It's been my curious friend at the cross who helps me better understand the simplicity of prayer. It's the admirer at the cross who reminds me that I am here once again for repentance. I laugh at myself, for I came for one thing, and with my judgmental thoughts toward the admirer I stay to repent of yet another.

If you're an admirer or curious, a brought-up Christian or a prodigal child, Jesus is seeking you. He's right here, right now. He is the way, the truth, and the life. Nothing in the whole world gets better than knowing He loves you and you can love Him back. Don't stay lost or consumed by the crowd any longer.

I'm so glad Jesus takes me just as I am. Translating Jesus means we do this for others. Didn't do what you hoped to do in that conversation or that interaction? Wish that person could have heard this or didn't hear that? Speak the language of Christ and pray for God to keep working and for that person to be open to the love of the Father.

Prompting.

Love someone who is not like you.

11 Step into Stories

Ben and I had ventured out to the coastline for an afternoon hike in Hawaii. I was curious as to what three young women up ahead were looking at in the waters below. As we drew near, they began pointing out the largest turtles we'd ever seen. While we looked down in awe, one of the women spoke up.

"Are you Ben? Ben Pilgreen?"

We both gave her a puzzled look and a smile as we tried to place her.

"You baptized me!" she shouted over the trade winds. "In Tuscaloosa."

Yes! When this woman—Mari—was a college student at the University of Alabama in 2007, Ben baptized her. Clearly, we were all shocked and excited and amazed. This was not normal. We hadn't seen her in almost fifteen years. Mari enthusiastically translated the story to her two schoolteacher friends while Ben and I tried to center our spinning minds.

God gets all the credit for this reunion. He put Mari on this edge of coastline on this particular summer afternoon and sent His turtles to keep her enthralled long enough for us to get there.

Do you see it? Everyone is important. Everything we do, big or small, for the kingdom of God matters. If you're doubting if what you are doing today matters, look at the people God has put in front of you and know it does. Ben and I needed this moment. We needed to be reminded, as silly as it sounds, that God is still using us, and as people come in and out of our lives, they don't exit the kingdom of God! Let's step into their stories whether they are open or closed. Let's go and make friends with strangers.

Awkward is a given.

This is the page you've been looking for. You'll find yourself here. *Evangelism* isn't your favorite word in the Christian language. It's the least of your gifts. In fact, you keep it in the emergency kit and pray you'll never have to use it on anyone . . . that another Christian will get there first. Evangelism can make for an awkward Christian. And awkward Christians come in all varieties.

Instead of wondering who the awkward are, let's just call us what we *all* are at times: awkward, embarrassed, graceless. We can be inwardly awkward with our ping-ponging thoughts of *should have, could have, didn't,* and *don't.* We fumble over our words. We're not good at sharing our faith. We're awkward because we want to be intellectual and winsome in our speech, but we feel foolish as we dodge or get flattened by hard questions and stumble around the subject.

I think of the times I've been awkward as I dodge hard spiritual questions. I also turn awkward when I'm asked by non-Christians what I write about or what I do in our city. I am still awkward. I don't like that to still be true, but when your flesh and the Spirit occupy the same square footage of a human body, it can only get awkward.

But *awkward* is how marriage proposals happen. It's why athletes do crazy moves after they make a great play. It explains the crowd's response when their band takes the stage. People will be all kinds of awkward if the motivation is compelling enough.

I think awkward is needed—yes, necessary—for us to become bilingual. It might feel this way to you because it's a new and different engagement, with intentionality and thought. It will be quite refreshing, though, to those who feel loved and heard, seen and valued by you. If you never experience an awkward conversation or have awkward moments where you wonder if you just screwed everything up, I'm not sure you've ever shared your Jesus story with someone. People want to know you're real and genuine and not gimmicky. I'm not hating on Christians, but we really can be a weird bunch. Sometimes it is legit that our cultures and contexts can't understand us. Other times we bring it upon ourselves, and to the non-Christians who take notice, I'm sorry.

Take notice of the man who awkwardly reentered society, returning to a people who have lived afraid of him. They were used to his nakedness, homelessness, anger, and fits. Just because Jesus set him free from demon possession and restored his sanity didn't mean everyone else would welcome him back. The man knew that much, and he preferred to leave with Jesus and His disciples. But Jesus told him, "Go home to your own people and tell them how much the Lord has done for you, and how he has had mercy on you" (Mark 5:19 NIV). Can you imagine how awkward this had to be for everyone? Yet the man obeyed, and awkward proved to be amazing!

One time, I was in and out of sleep on an international flight when I felt a tap on the shoulder. I peered between the seats to discover an airplane napkin being handed to me. *What in the world?*

It read in blue ink: "Hi. I'm stalling a little but the Holy Spirit said to ask you how to write books. Are you an author?"

I read it about eighty-seven times. Then I woke up Ben and had him read it. Who knew what the napkin writer was thinking. Probably telling herself it was a bad idea. Meanwhile, I was having an out-of-body experience thirty thousand feet over the ocean. The obvious answer to her question was yes, but that didn't seem to suffice in the moment.

I awkwardly squeezed my face between the seats and told her yes. She covered her face. What was happening? I stayed in that uncomfortable position and waited. I watched her wipe away tears. Her body shook. I noticed a little hand comfort her shoulder. She then gripped that little hand and looked at me.

"I knew it. But this is all new to me." Her smile was more beautiful than the Italian landscape we had just left. "God has prompted me before, but I never know if it's my crazy idea or His. I went out on a limb here," she shared.

We were both recipients of this most delightful mystery of stepping into stories. How did God place us both here at this moment? Her name was Remi, and she was traveling back to Georgia from Uganda, where she and her three kids had spent time with family. Ben and I were returning from a trip of a lifetime to Italy with our best friends.

Strangers aren't that strange.

When you sit down to eat at a restaurant in town, you are physically in your culture and have the chance to step into so many stories. When you pray with eyes either open or closed for those in the restaurant, you are using the language of Christ. And you can use that language over your culture by praying for the owners, servers, and customers present in the room. Restaurants have the potential to be the most prayed over places in culture! One day my friend and I asked our server if we could pray for anything specific for her. She said she wanted more love and peace in her life. But before we could start our prayer, in a childlike way she pulled up a chair from an empty table nearby to join us. This is the land we're called to engage. Be present. Be attentive. Be there. Everywhere we go on every piece of land, whether we call it sacred or secular, belongs to God. (And let restaurant workers know we are Christians by our love in the form of generous tips.)

When you are in the waiting room at the doctor's office, you are physically in your culture. Everyone there is facing something. You can pray for that little girl to be brave, offer comfort to that older man, and let that mother with multiple children know she's doing a good job. And ask for God to work His power in your own circumstances.

We are standing on the same soil anyway. Jesus engaged with the thief as they both bled on crosses. He was friends with prostitutes, tax collectors, and fishermen. To befriend poor, rejected, and unexpected people is to understand Jesus. You will hear Him as you walk your streets, meet with Him, and pray for your people.

Conversation unlocks friendships that the world deems impossible to form. Bonhoeffer reminds us that "[Jesus] confronts you in every person that you meet. Christ walks on the earth as your neighbor as long as there are people."[1] So let's work on being winsome because of our faith, not being weird about our faith.

You play a part in the stories of others. You can be a Christian witness for a young person who will then go to college and be invited to go to church—and they remember you and say yes to the invitation. You can be a parent in the preschool play group or watching a soccer game from the sidelines and bring truth and hope to another parent. You have the conversation in you that your coworker needs to hear about purpose.

You'll recall Christine, Tiffany, Dion, and three international college students at the gate in chapter 4. Here they are at the cross. Christine was curious about God, came to church, and met a small group of families who were in a similar life stage. This was all so new to her Taiwanese and atheistic upbringing. Then came a cancer scare. For several months, this small group would tuck in their kids and then hop on a video call to hear her latest medical report and pray for her. She opened herself up to new people who stepped into her story.

The week of Tiffany's birthday was a time each year she was often hard on herself, questioning her existence and purpose. Her long text to me one morning called for a chocolate intervention. On her birthday, Dandelion Chocolate was the spot we chose to meet. We were in very different life stages and had little in common, except I happened to be present as she was coming to the end of herself and needed to talk about it.

Dion drives bus 44 in my city. Before he gets behind the steering wheel and maneuvers all over San Francisco, he places his hands on the bus and prays. Dion and I both know he gets quite a few characters on his daily route. He hears all kinds of conversations and can't help but wonder about people's stories as they board the bus. Every stranger who steps onto that bus has been prayed for by their bus driver.

Nino, Nikole, and Alli moved to another country after their brief stay in my city. I wondered if I had shown my curious friends enough of the love of Jesus. I wondered if what they experienced in our church community was compelling enough for them to find another church community in their new country. I wondered if Jesus was just another great teacher they'd learn from along life's journey. Then I got a text from Nikole. After a few weeks of being away from Christian community, she found home again at a new church in her new country.

Is the door open or closed?

The stories I shared are moments when the doors are open, when people are receptive, when you are trying to both listen and speak Christ and culture. **If the door is open, talk to them about Jesus.**

Don't ignore that prompting you sense to talk about Jesus. My friend Jess is a Christian living in Boulder, Colorado, and as she lets the Holy Spirit work in her, she teaches me what she observes. "Regarding the Holy Spirit, we want the filling without the yielding. We often want an increase of the Holy Spirit in our lives—an outpouring of miracles, healings, spiritual awakenings, eyes to see, ears to hear—but when He asks us to do the smallest things in our daily lives, we are quick to ignore Him because it doesn't feel big enough."

Cornelius was an Italian prayer warrior. He was listening to God in prayer one day and got a vision to bring Peter, one of Christ's original twelve disciples, to his home. Peter was living several hours away and was also praying and received a vision, except he got one he couldn't understand. Up to this point in history, Jews and non-Jews didn't associate with one another. Cornelius was respected by the Jewish people though he was a non-Jew. It's important to be respected among the people you want to reach and enjoy fellowship with. Our relationships are also extremely fragile on the front end. When Peter showed up at Cornelius's home, God showed him that though culture said he shouldn't be there, God said he should (Acts 10:28, 34–35)!

What good is God doing in your life? What is something hard and challenging you are facing, but you know God is with you? I believe it's often what God is doing in us in the waiting and silence that turns out to be the best thing we can offer our friends by way of encouragement. Zechariah and Elizabeth shared the good news of their son's birth with their neighbors, and this caused their neighbors to share in the joy. It was more personal than that, as Zechariah did so out of what God had been doing in his heart during his months of silence.

Help people see Jesus around them. When you listen to their stories, invite them to consider God's presence. Prod with questions: "Do you think this might be God getting your attention?" "Where do you think this love comes from?" "What is your identity wrapped up in?" "Why do you think you are on this earth?" "How have you been able to accomplish what you have thus far?" Pay attention to God-tracing in chapter 14.

If the door is closed, talk to Jesus about them. While you're listening to culture, the Holy Spirit is speaking to you concerning culture. Not all doors are open, and the pictures I painted in the stories before were not smooth and easy in real life. As we pay attention to culture and its ever-changing ways, we are mindful in prayer and sensitive to the Spirit's activity. We are creatively thinking with His mind on how to engage various cultural situations. Just because we live in this world doesn't mean our engagement has to be done like this world.

Remember Charleston at Marshalls? I didn't tell you that story because I've got it all figured out. I tell you that story because I'm learning how to recognize open and closed doors and then proceed with love.

Before I stepped into the store that day, I had another encounter. As I crossed Mission and 4th, I heard loud and crazy noises. When I turned to look, I saw a man dragging a blanket around in circles in the intersection. Unfortunately, this didn't shock anyone around, but it should sadden us all. We cannot be okay with this.

I'm learning to voice the name of Jesus out loud toward a situation or person I can't approach. This takes discernment, and what I speak of are moments where safety comes first. As busy and distracted as everyone was, I didn't look out of place praying out loud.

Jesus, You love this man. He is made in Your image. This is not the plan You have for him. In the power of Your name, set him free. Free him from whatever it is that is holding him captive. There is power in Your name, and I've read about it in the New Testament. Come and do it again in and for this man.

I believe he calmed down. Was this a prayer answered? Was he just physically exhausted from shouting? Regardless, for his sake I was grateful. I kept walking and ended up in Marshalls.

These encounters don't happen to me every day, but they are becoming more common. Jesus has a thing for doors. After the resurrection, He would just appear on the other side of a locked door. He still does this with His followers today! As you pay attention to the people in your specific context and pray to God on their behalf, you'll be continuously interrupted and invited into stories you know are of the Holy Spirit. (I'll lead you on how to pray on the spot, pray about what you see, and let the Spirit speak through you in the next chapter.)

Paul said it best to the church in Colossae (in modern-day Turkey) as he wrote to encourage the Christ followers not to get caught up with earthly pursuits but to live for Christ.

Continue steadfastly in prayer, being watchful in it with thanksgiving. At the same time, pray also for [Christ followers], that God may open to us a door for the word, to declare the mystery of Christ . . . that I may make it clear, which is how I ought to speak. Walk in wisdom toward outsiders, making the best use of the time. Let your speech always be gracious, seasoned with salt, so that you may know how you ought to answer each person. (Col. 4:2–6)

If it's an open door, go in. If it's a closed door, pray. Regardless, a Spirit-filled life is an active life.

Prompting.

Be brave and confident. You've got nothing to lose, and they have everything to gain.

12 Practice the Language

Harriet Tubman couldn't read or write, but she could pray. That language proved invaluable. She even prayed for her enslaver to find Jesus so he would change his ways. Her prayers intensified as she made nineteen trips to bring over three hundred people with God-given souls to freedom. "Oh, Lord, You've been with me in six troubles, don't desert me in the seventh!" she'd pray. "She talked with God, and He talked with her every day of her life . . . for she said she never ventured only where God sent her."[1] She wasn't just communicating with Jesus. She was frequently reasoning with her people to pursue freedom. "Hers was not a religion of a morning and evening prayer at stated times, but when she felt a need, she simply told God about it, and trusted Him to set the matter right."[2]

I want to talk to Jesus like Harriet talked to Jesus. I want to talk to my people like Harriet talked to her people. Every soul matters. Every conversation with Jesus makes a difference. The language of Christ is talking and listening to Jesus. He is alive, and we get to have conversations with Him. I don't naturally think to pray like this in my day. Nothing of this chapter is natural. Let's bring the practical and partner with the Holy Spirit to blow in the supernatural.

We've talked about giving structure to the language of Christ with prayer, Scripture, and the Holy Spirit, and now this chapter will equip us to put them into practice as we work to become bilingual among our people. It is here at the cross where we bridge what our people know and love to what Jesus knows and loves. If they love science, bring up creation and how we're always thinking God's thoughts after Him as we explore this world. If they are caring for their aging parent, ask how they see God's provision and grace in their parent's face. Also think about what of your story is compelling, current, and relatable. Practice sharing that.

Whether you are a brand-new Christian or longtime Christ follower, if you know and obey, then because Jesus is enough, anything you say about Him is enough. Remember, prayer is the language of Christ. Attentiveness is the language of culture. I want to show you how this language rises off the pages of Scripture, as we read the Word, and into your voice and vocabulary. Talk to Jesus about people through prayer walking and prayer stacking. Pray on the spot as often as you can. Don't worry about the result. That part is not ultimately up to you anyway.

Talk to Jesus about them.

Because you've paid attention at the gate, you want to pray. Because you see Jesus at the gate and have encountered Him at the cross, you are able to pray. Turn what you see into what you pray. **This is praying *for* people.** To practice the language of Christ, you have to pray. I've never met someone who articulates they are great at prayer. Because we communicate with a great and mysterious God, His followers will always be learning new and different ways to share our praise, our burdens, and our confessions with Him. Three tips from the Alpha Course on how to pray are to keep it simple, keep it honest, and keep it going.[3] I love how this approach takes the mechanics out of prayer and keeps it as an ongoing conversation with Jesus, where we pick up where we left off and where He always has our ear! As Christ brings things to our attention, He wants us to stay on topic and pray about what He gives us to see, what He gives us to think, and who He leads us to love.

God's eyes are roaming this earth looking for those whose hearts are fully committed to Him (2 Chron. 16:9). That's who He wants to use. That's who He needs standing in the gap (Ezek. 22:30). Let's put feet to our faith, action to our aching, and intercession to our intuition. Now is the time to make our voices heard to God. Jesus knows this season better than anyone. He stepped into a world with high tensions, political unrest, scarce finances, low trust, and dwindling expectations for the coming Messiah. Yet Jesus chose to live among us, to learn our names and stories, and to start conversations about what was heavy on our minds. Our communities need people who will first offer prayers of praise, intercession, thanksgiving, and confession.

Prayer walking is just what it sounds like: to intentionally go on a walk for the purpose of prayer. This can be during your lunch break or the last few minutes of your morning run. While you're strolling with your kids around the park, you can pray for everyone you see. You can invite others to go on a walk and pray together.

Here is a suggestion of ten places to pray and what you can pray for:

1. Home (family)
2. Church (more of Jesus)
3. City hall (community)
4. Police station (safety)
5. School (learning)
6. Hospital (healing)
7. Neighborhood/street (unity)
8. Neglected areas (needs met)
9. Businesses (commerce)
10. City limit signs/boundaries/bridges (what comes in and out of town; what brings people in and out)

John Stott suggested we "begin by speaking back to God on the same subject on which he has spoken to you. Don't change the conversation!"[4] You may step into stories via prayer that you'll never step into via life. Our prayers can cause things not to happen and can unleash God's power to do the impossible.

Sometimes we meet resistance when we pray because we pray. Here are four things to do when you meet resistance:

1. Meet with God about it. When people don't want you to talk to them, talk to God about them for now.
2. Prayer walk around places of influence. You want the evil plans disrupted in town? Go prayer walk places of resistance. You want truth to be taught and encouragement given at school? Prayer walk around the schools. You want to see change happen at city hall and in the courthouse but feel defeated and like you're swimming upstream? Prayer walk around these places of influence.

3. Pray for signs and look for signs. "God, give me eyes to see and ears to hear." Then, in boldness and humility, do something with what you see and hear.

4. Prayer stack. Prayer stacking is when someone prays over a place or intercedes for someone, and then another person comes behind them and prays in agreement with those prayers. Invite others to prayer stack with you. We have joined dozens of families and prayed circles around future homes and schools and doctors' offices. We will take a day and invite others to prayer walk certain streets and ask God to work specifically against any evil at work or for the breakthrough we are desperate to see.

Friends, my encouragement and challenge to us all is to not absorb any resistance we encounter but to release love in that space and in this place. It's not easy, but we're not called to easy. We're called to Jesus, who met the greatest resistance—the sin in all of humanity—and conquered death to give us His love and freedom to share with others. Let us be challenged by Dietrich Bonhoeffer, someone who met resistance often: "Interaction with God must be practiced; otherwise we will not find the right language when he surprises us. . . . We must learn God's language, laboriously learn it. And we must work at it, so that we will be able to talk with him."[5]

Pray on the spot.

Perhaps you still resist because you don't like to pray out loud, or the thought to pray doesn't even occur to you while you're out and about. Pause a minute here, right now. Voice a prayer in your heart for what you see. For me, as I write this, it's midday, and everyone in the coffee shop around me is desperate for caffeine if we are to continue for a few more hours.

Father, direct their steps to You. Give them thoughts of Your love. Lead them to encounters of Your grace.

I notice the barista looks at me as I look around. *She knows. She's figured me out!* Okay, maybe she hasn't, but it is awesome if she has. I smile at her and get back to writing.

Prayer on the spot is often one-on-one prayer with another person. Talking to Jesus, well, that's between the two of you, and He understands ideas and thoughts in your head that you can't quite formulate into words. The Holy Spirit speaking through you when you pray? This takes faith, and once it happens, you'll want Him to do it again. We can be fully human before Christ in prayer because He was fully human before us on the cross.

If Jesus matters to you, and you believe He can do anything, then your heart is turned toward Him and that's where your prayers start. It's never what you pray but to whom you pray. If your heart is after Jesus, everything else will come. He tells us to seek Him first and everything will be added. He also says if we ask, seek, and knock, the door will be opened (Matt. 7:7). Turn your heart to start. **This is actually praying *with* people.**

It's common Christian language to say, "I'm praying for you." Someone shares a concern or burden, and you tell them you'll pray for them. Later, you actually pray for their need. But praying on the spot is different. It invites the presence of God into our midst immediately because we pray right then, right there.

At church, Mary shared with me the stress of house hunting, her mom's heart condition, and a friend's terminal diagnosis.

We prayed together on the spot. She didn't just know I loved her but also felt the love of Jesus come upon her. When she texted midweek that they'd gotten a house, I didn't have to wonder how it happened. We got to praise God together!

Dan had a few job offers and couldn't decide. In addition to talking about the options, Ben and Dan prayed together over the phone.

Jan was traveling to Texas to visit her mom. She's open to all types of positive thinking. I asked via a text if I could pray with her. I literally typed out the prayer and shared it with her. Jan might not believe in Jesus yet, but she read what He's capable of and what I'm believing Him for!

I'm learning my unbelieving friends will reuse the prayers I share with them. They haven't opened themselves up to a relationship with Jesus yet, so they will borrow my faith and my prayers. I believe Jesus considers this a part of their journey and meets them where they are, just like He met me where I was.

We have not because we ask not! It will shock people and catch them off guard to bring prayer into a conversation. You are inviting in God's presence. Those in the midst of prayer will not be more mad or angry after the prayer. If anything, they will feel more peaceful, and we will feel more real to them.

It's not you anyway.

Not everyone had faith in Harriet Tubman or thought the risky chance of escape worthwhile. I imagine she used few words to convince others to leave their families and livelihoods behind. Her actions spoke love. They either stayed behind or made the dangerous journey with her. Every person we translate Jesus to has the same two options: to follow Him or stay where they are. We do our part in prayer and partnership with Jesus. He is still the one who saves and works His mysterious miracles. I've used the word *magic* at the gate, for that's what culture calls it, but Christ calls kingdom work *miraculous*. Magic has no attachment and is reproducible, just like coffee, chai, and strawberry daiquiris. Miracles have an origin, and every one is a unique story.

The way we learn the language of Christ is through Scripture, prayer, and the Holy Spirit. Philip spoke the language of Christ to the Ethiopian eunuch (Acts 8:26–39). Paul went outside the gate to the riverside to pray, and the Lord opened up Lydia's heart to pay attention to him (16:13–15). The purpose of this chapter, of this book, is to encourage practice. We tell what we know and what we've personally experienced with Jesus. No one can argue with our stories, and no one can deny the power of the Holy Spirit in these conversations.

Think of it like this: we want our kids to learn from us and then put those lessons to work in their lives. We want this for others too: not just to hear us but to put our words into practice. We want this for our sports teams, master classes, and what we're learning as a human race. We want to receive knowledge, to be educated, and then to use that knowledge to make the world a better place. Why stop and hesitate on practicing Jesus's teachings?

Is it possible that because we've got other philosophies, other systems, and our own selves in our heads, we aren't able to fully grasp the truths of Jesus? We can do what we read Jesus did, what we have seen Him do in others, and what other disciples have done for centuries. What have you seen Jesus do? Do you believe the same power that the first disciples had to heal the sick, cast out demons, and teach repentance is available to you?

I clean my face like I watched my mom clean her face when I was a little girl. I pack our van the way I've watched my dad pack our van since childhood. I even wear red lipstick occasionally because of my friend Bea. So much of life is put into practice by what we've been taught.

What have you seen Jesus do that you can do? I've seen how He loves me and forgives me and still loves me. I've experienced His peace in hard times. Jesus has helped me find joy when my circumstances have been anything but joyful. I can love. I can forgive. I can be a peaceful presence in someone's life. I can voice words of encouragement and prayer and Scripture to a friend who is in hard circumstances. Jesus sends us out to do what He can do, and He can do anything!

The Holy Spirit takes you to places you can't believe. Are you ready to talk to people about the hope you have with gentleness and respect? Turn what you hear in your spirit into what you say with your mouth. This is God speaking through you. No matter whom you are speaking with, no matter their knowledge of spiritual things, "the Holy Spirit will teach you in that very hour what you ought to say" (Luke 12:12). At another time, when Jesus's followers were together and the Holy Spirit came upon them, "they started speaking in a number of different languages as the Spirit prompted them" (Acts 2:4 Message).

German pastor Christoph Blumhardt, who spoke during Nazi times, said, "We must speak in practical terms. Either Christ's coming has meaning for us now, or else it means nothing at all."[6]

I met Ernie when he came by to look at our roof. He returned with his supervisor, and while his supervisor was filling out the paperwork, I learned Ernie's story of moving to California from Armenia when he was in fourth grade, and how they'd left suddenly in the middle of the night. He asked about our move to California. I told him we'd moved here to plant a church. "My wife is very religious, but I am not. I respect her views and values very much," he said. I asked him what kept him away from Jesus. He said he didn't want to be a hypocrite, and he knew who he was didn't align with who Jesus was. One day, a few weeks later, Ernie returned to pick up our payment and final paperwork. I learned that his uncle, who'd helped them leave his home country, had passed away since the last time Ernie was at our house. Ernie and I had already discussed him feeling like he had to work some things out before he could come to God. I encouraged him that Jesus takes us just like we are.

"He loves you, Ernie. Like your girls came to you early on—they needed you and had little to give you but their love. Something happens one day, and they see they've got something to give back to you to show their thanks. Ernie, right now, you can be needy with Jesus. Come to Him for love, forgiveness, comfort, and peace. Just tell Him what you need. He's got it. A day is coming when you'll realize you've got something to give to Him. For now, let Jesus love you. When that gets you, you'll want to love Him back."

Prompting.

Wherever you are reading this, who do you see that you can pray for on the spot? Go and speak a blessing to them—yes, to the stranger.

13 Read the Scriptures

Our minds are at war with what we actually believe. *Why am I on this earth? Am I even making a difference? Where is God, and why is there so much evil? Does God still care? Can I trust Him?* Even Christians who have followed Jesus for many years still ask these questions. Research shows we have over six thousand thoughts per day.[1] One thought leads to another, or we second-guess a thought we had earlier.

Are the good and truthful Scriptures even a contestant in this mental war? People are dying for truth. Are we even living for it? If His Word is not in us, God cannot use it as a translation tool. If it is, He promises through His Spirit to draw from His Word as we speak. Many Christians don't share the life-changing news of Jesus because it doesn't matter enough to them, or we don't speak as ones who have met with Him and His Word today.

Let me stir you by way of another reminder that people are hungry for truth. You adding to a conversation or sending in a text what hope you read in your Bible today might save someone's life. Sharing what Jesus has done for you today in itself is enough to change the heart of the least likely—someone who you think is the furthest from God that is humanly possible. And we all have this person in our lives.

Brian has all the facts, but the resurrection seems highly unlikely to him. I wonder if he'll ever believe. Ernie feels like he's too hypocritical to come to Jesus. Jan would have to give up her way of life to follow Jesus, and that doesn't look likely. Saul, later known as the apostle Paul, was highly unlikely to follow Jesus, looking at his track record. But aren't we all? Every human is one decision away from giving their life to Jesus.

I refuse to live afraid to share my faith with others because I'm not sure what to say, how to say it, or how it will be received. If love is my motivation, if the Bible is daily getting in me, then it's the Holy Spirit who does the transforming as I do the translating. Remember, we are of the company of enthusiastic witnesses.

Who are we if we don't have our language? Pastor Andy Stanley's explanation in his Investigating Jesus series is a great reminder of the impact of Scripture. To summarize, there was an event called the resurrection that instituted the first century and led to a movement in which documents were written. Three hundred years later, the Bible was assembled, thanks to Emperor Constantine, who lifted the ban against Christianity and allowed those first-century documents to come out. Stanley points out that the very Roman Empire that crucified Jesus was the same empire that financed the assembly of the first Bibles.[2]

People who don't know and love Jesus would naturally consider the cross of Christ foolishness. The concern in my writing is for those who are being saved. We—who never arrive and are always being converted—read the Scriptures because we are still being formed. Followers can't go long without meditating and reading His Word. Jesus is that approachable and attractive.

The Bible is for you.

I know when I act in rebellion to my Savior and look to the cross and to the Christ whom I owe my life, I'm not who I could be if left to myself, nor am I yet complete. He's changed me. But if, in my prayers, God will grow my love for you and my neighbors, I am on my way to His likeness.

Edith Stein wrote,

> In the childhood of the spiritual life, when we have just begun to allow ourselves to be directed by God, we feel his guiding hand quite firmly and surely. But it doesn't always stay that way. Whoever belongs to Christ must go the whole way with him.[3]

We need His truth in us, and not just by way of Sunday gatherings and Christian teachers and media channels. If we believe Jesus is the truth, we will figure out a way to regularly read the Book of Truth. New Testament writer John, one of Jesus's beloved followers, wrote a few things about this. He said that Jesus has always been around and will always be the Word, and He was the same Word when He put on flesh to live on earth. John quotes Jesus in saying He is the way, the truth, and the life, and if we abide in Him and let His words abide in us, we can ask for anything in prayer and it will be done (John 1:1; 14:6; 15:7). To be a current follower of Jesus is to be reading the Bible on a regular basis. To be an out-of-date follower is to have to remember something you've read a while back.

Father, make Your living Word precious to us again.

Jesus has left us His Word and His Spirit. The Bible helps us better explain our faith. It is a written, accessible, historical document that people can tangibly encounter and determine for themselves if they believe. Through it, anyone who reads its God-breathed words can experience the unleashing of the Holy Spirit to unlock mystery, open eyes, and reveal truth.

Let the reading of the Holy Scriptures in, and let the Holy Spirit change you. When my friend Chris began to consider the Bible as God's love letter to her, it changed how she read it and how often she read it. Christ's disciples who read the Bible have the Holy Spirit guiding us into mystery and truth and understanding. When you read the Bible, invite the Holy Spirit to help you understand. Reading Scripture with the Holy Spirit is like having the Author read His own audiobook with commentary!

For Christians to translate Jesus, we must know Scripture. Why is this a challenge? Why is this not as important as eating, sleeping, and working? If we got God's Word in us daily before we rolled out of bed or got going for the day, or before we greeted anyone else, how would we be changed?

> The Bible keeps us alive. Because the Scriptures are "living and active," as they get into us, they keep our souls alive (Heb. 4:12).
>
> The Bible keeps us from sinning. As we read it, we learn which ways to walk and what pitfalls to avoid (Ps. 119:10–11).
>
> If we meditate on the Word "day and night," we will have a successful life (Josh. 1:8).
>
> Everything written in the Bible gives us hope (Rom. 15:4).
>
> Knowing the Bible "[makes us] wise" (2 Tim. 3:15).

Every word of the Bible "is breathed out by God" (2 Tim. 3:16).

The Bible has everything we need to be "equipped for every good work" (2 Tim. 3:17).

The Bible keeps us ready to answer. The Lord told Jeremiah, "Get yourself ready! Stand up and say to them whatever I command you" (Jer. 1:17 NIV).

The Bible keeps us hydrated. The challenge is that Christians are dehydrated and don't know it. They are grabbing intoxicating drinks at the cultural counter. Their lips are chapped. Their souls are having to pull from bodily reserves to keep alive (Isa. 55:1–3).

When will we wake up and realize His Word is "more precious than gold [and] . . . sweeter than honey" (Ps. 19:10 NIV)?

The Bible is for the least likely.

"Meanwhile, the witnesses laid their coats at the feet of a young man named Saul" (Acts 7:58 NIV). *Meanwhile,* because at the same time the guys were getting riled up as they dragged Stephen outside of the Lion's Gate. "And Saul approved of their killing him. . . . [He] began to destroy the church. Going from house to house, he dragged off both men and women and put them in prison" (8:1, 3 NIV). As Philip was translating Jesus to an Ethiopian eunuch, "Meanwhile [at the same time again], Saul was still breathing out murderous threats against the Lord's disciples. He went to the high priest and asked him for letters . . . so that if he found any there who belonged to the Way . . . he might take them as prisoners" (9:1–2 NIV).

What were the chances Saul, of all people, would become one of Jesus's main translators for the first century? Saul was a young student of God's law but not a student of God's love. He knew of the Old Testament prophets, kings, and priests. He was surrounded by a growing number of Jesus followers. He could see the way the disciples were serving. He would hear them tell stories.

Saul loved insurrections. He stirred up crowds. He made up lies as he went along. He went after churches. His passion took him door-to-door. The Lord's disciples kept him up at night. Saul was convinced he was helping God out by ending the movement of Jesus. If love is not our motivation, then our motivation has not come from God.

Saul then left Jerusalem fully intending to return with Christ followers as his prisoners. Instead, Jesus literally stopped him and got his attention, and Saul became Paul, transformed by Jesus and full of the Holy Spirit. When he encountered Jesus on the road to Damascus and experienced the Holy Spirit, Paul came alive. Paul traveled the world establishing Christian communities. He took the Good News to Greece, Turkey, Italy, and possibly Spain. He wrote much of the New Testament. No matter where Paul was—in prison, on boats, in city squares or homes, he took every possible opportunity to bring the language of love into every conversation.

Let reading the Bible move you to pray and obey. Stephen read the Bible. The truth got in him, and then it affected Saul and kept the disciples in Damascus safe. It affected Philip and inspired his conversation with the Ethiopian eunuch. Someone is watching the effects of Scripture in your life. Saul, with his hardened heart, had widened eyes to see how the Lord's disciples were living. He knew they were taking care of the widows and orphans. He saw how they greeted one another in Jerusalem. He could tell they really believed in this man named Jesus. He heard what Stephen said about his ancestor Moses. Saul was aware of the effects of Scripture in the lives of Jesus's disciples, even as he considered himself the least likely to become one.

There are things we cannot do for others, but I've read my Bible enough to know there are things we can do. We can invite God's presence into a room. We can speak emboldened by His Spirit. We can show love.

Elizabeth is a young professional living in New York. Her scriptural wisdom is growing as she studies the Bible on a regular basis both on her own and in community. She's not necessarily sharing what she's reading in her Bible to her colleagues during office hours. She also feels like she can't keep up with the cultural talk they are consumed with. She's picking up enough culture by living in it. Truth is, her scriptural wisdom is affecting everything she thinks and does. We must count biblical knowledge as the highest wisdom revealed to humankind.

Your friend, coworker, family member, or neighbor might be the least likely, but let that not hold you back. Love was not Saul's motivation until Jesus met him. Then Saul was changed to Paul and his conversion began. Let love flow out. Intercede. Serve. Whatever you do, don't rule anyone out. God hasn't left that up to His people.

Do something with your Bible.

Only 11 percent of Americans read the Bible daily in a country where 65 percent claim to be Christians.[4] People don't read it because they don't understand it or don't know when or how to use it. We will raise an illiterate generation if we make the Bible optional in the Christian faith. It is becoming one of many voices instead of the voice of truth. We think parts of the Bible strange when what is truly strange is that Jesus followers haven't fully read the manual associated with their faith. Would more people consider Jesus if Christians did something with their Bibles daily?

Daily, yes. If that is asking too much, join the disciples who could no longer follow Jesus. Jesus said in Luke 9:23 that following Him is a daily practice. If we can drink a glass of water to stay hydrated, we can put His Word into us to stay connected. However long it takes to consume all 31,102 verses, drink from it often. If it takes eighty-five years or two years to read all of it, how different you will be with His truth flowing through you!

I thought the Bible meant something to me until I emptied out a backpack full of them in Guangzhou, China, and watched as older ladies began to use all their strength to tear them apart. Without a second thought, as if they'd done this before, they made each single book into many books. What was precious to me was far more precious to them. I realized in that moment that I treated the Bible as something for my convenience, while these ladies treated it as something priceless and sharable.

It was on this college mission trip experience to China that I met Pastor Samuel Lamb.[5] He was a high-profile pastor, so the government wouldn't do much to him, but he went to prison twice, the second time for over twenty years, and his father and wife died while he was incarcerated. He was considered an anti-revolutionist because he preached about Jesus. The illegal house church he led grew after he was released from prison. People filled the stairs and courtyard of the three-story building.

On the day we were there, the women made it their joy to tear up the thousand smuggled Bibles. "More people will have access to Jesus," was the message translated to us. Pastor Lamb then took us up to the third story and sat snug around a PVC pipe that went down through the floor. The pipe had holes made in it so that all those who gathered could hear him speak as they piled into the building several times a week.

This suffering, persecuted church was thriving. The government tried to rule them, imprison them, hurt them, take away their Bibles, and make their lives harder. Why would any government care about the Bible if it didn't have power? What do governments believe that Christians don't believe?

I left with a lighter backpack and a more convicted heart. I wanted to love Jesus like Pastor Lamb. I wanted the Bible to be precious to me like it was to my brothers and sisters in China.

Who doesn't want this? What in our world can ever match what the Scriptures promise? Everything our friends are looking for can all be found in Christ. But we as His followers must show a life that is being transformed as His Word is in us.

Christianity is an outlier. No other practice, religion, or system holds like it does. Everything will push against Christian beliefs because they can't align with it. *Following Jesus wouldn't be so hard if everyone else around me would make it easier!* Herein we see where our allegiance lies. Following Jesus and translating Him isn't easy. Disciples would hear what Jesus taught and decide to no longer follow Him. It's why He asked the Twelve, "You do not want to leave too, do you?" (John 6:67 NIV). Peter replied, and I wonder if you and I might give consideration to his answer. "Lord, to whom shall we go? You have the words of eternal life" (v. 68). Do you believe what Peter believed?

Life with Christ is anything but dull. If we find it dull, we've not truly explored the Christian faith, the castle of our souls. We've not let God in. We must follow Him around, for He has such good in store for us. Life with Jesus is exciting!

If ever we lose our fascination with Christ and His Word, we lose our effectiveness for Christ and His world. It's why we keep coming back to the gate, the cross, and the table. It's not a one-and-done thing with salvation. Christ's followers need the Spirit of God to understand the Bible, what God is doing in our world, and what He is telling us to do.

The Spirit takes the living Scriptures and works them out in our daily lives. As we open up the Bible, we pray,

Holy Spirit, teach me that I might understand the things "freely given [me] by God" (1 Cor. 2:12). When I speak, help me interpret/translate truths so that people's faith will not rest on me but on "the power of God" (vv. 4–5).

Our conversations won't be polished. They were never intended to be. Our brother Paul said any "eloquent wisdom" would take the spotlight off the cross of Christ, and that's what we want people to see (1 Cor. 1:17). Does the cross of Jesus Christ hold any power in your life? (v. 18).

I love the language Paul used to describe the Christians in Ephesus when they learned about Jesus and decided to put their trust in Him. "And you also were included in Christ when you heard the message of truth, the gospel of your salvation. When you believed, you were marked in him with a seal, the promised Holy Spirit" (Eph. 1:13 NIV). We are also included when we learn who Jesus is and what He has done for us. Do something with your Bible. Hear it. Read it. Believe it.

Prompting.

What is Jesus doing in the Bible today? Keep encountering Jesus in the Bible.

14 Connect with Christ and Culture

We all get to the cross of Jesus Christ on different paths. On that historic day, Simon of Cyrene carried Jesus's cross. The women walked mournfully together. The Roman soldiers treated the day's events as a joke. The two criminals hanging on their own crosses probably were the ones most pondering the actions that got them there. However everyone got to the cross that day, whatever they believed prior to that day, whomever they thought Jesus was, 100 percent of them could testify that Jesus Christ died. Testimonies from that day prove that Roman soldiers put their trust in Him. One of the criminals asked to be with Jesus in the afterlife. Everyone felt the earthquake. Everyone experienced something because of Christ's death that day, but not everyone believed in Him.

Richard is considering Jesus out of his ex-Mormon beliefs. Jesus came to Michael in a dream. Adrian found Jesus when his parents forsook him. Andrew lay in the hospital post-surgery pondering his purpose and reached for the Bible by his bed. Susan was strongly educated to believe Christianity and is re-thinking the claims of Christ from a perspective of love.

Maybe you've assumed that all people will come to know Jesus the same way you did. But people will come through logic, experience, trials, and revelation. They will come from having little exposure to religion or as they attempt to gather multiple values to form their own. We all get to Jesus on different paths. There's 360 degrees around the cross of Christ, yet it's Jesus, the Son of God, we all encounter.

How we get to Jesus will look different. How He chooses to reveal Himself to each of us will vary. One thing remains the same: Jesus is the Savior of the world and is the only way to God. There is only one Jesus, and it's in His name we are saved. We don't end up Christian or have a spiritual encounter that saves us. Jesus saves, and we each make a decision to receive His salvation or not.

Remember, disciples are students of Christ and culture. He is not just for those who believe but for all humanity. When we engage with culture, Christianity is intended to get stronger. I love Jesus more after my chats with Monty, after chai with the girls, and after front step exchanges with Jack and Anna. It is out of love we translate Jesus. It is through prayer, Scripture, and the Holy Spirit we connect to Christ and culture. In chapter 7, I proposed a framework for conversations about Jesus: Go narrow. Go through. Go wide. In this chapter, I suggest a few more practices as we become bilingual: Ask questions like Jesus. Trace people's steps back to Him. Love Jesus and let the world observe such devotion.

Ask the world questions.

We can ask questions with confidence because God is ahead. He is a forward-thinking God. I quoted Johannes Kepler at the gate, but his words bear repeating here: "I was merely thinking God's thoughts after him."[1] Culture is the one changing to try to figure things out. Culture makes us think that if we can't keep up with its constantly shifting viewpoints and thoughts, then we're behind.

We are ahead if we are with God. Christians are called into His truth. He is the same yesterday, today, and forever, which makes it easier to ask the world questions since He doesn't change (Mal. 3:6). It's easy to watch culture change and think that living out our faith makes us the outdated ones. Christ's followers haven't figured it all out either, because we see in the same dimension as everyone else, yet our faith in a steadfast God gives us glimpses beyond the here and now.

The world asks Christians questions to figure out what we believe. Do we ask the world questions to figure out what they believe?

How did Christ speak? He asked questions. I've learned from Martin Copenhaver's book *Jesus Is the Question* that He asked 307 different questions and was asked 183, of which He only answered a few. Asking questions was what Jesus did. Answering, not so much.[2]

There are many questions from the Bible that we can ask anyone. We ask because we love this world, not because we've got Jesus figured out. I find that when I ask the world questions, I realize how far I still have to go to know Jesus more, and this brings comfort to my non-Christian friends. Asking questions confirms we're students, learners, and followers.

In chapter 11, we learned to determine if the door of conversation is open or closed. Christians tend to be shy in an effort to avoid offense. However, when we sincerely care for people, we ask questions to better understand one another.

Do you believe God exists?

If you pray, who do you pray to?

Would you want to believe that there is someone more powerful and more in control than you?

What keeps you away from God?

What if you knew in your story that someone suffered for you to lead to a better story than you can write?[3]

The following questions derive from the Gospels:

What are you looking for? (John 1:38)

Who do you think Jesus is? (Mark 8:27)

What do you want Him to do for you? (Matt. 20:32)

Why are you so afraid? (Mark 4:40)

Since Jesus speaks truth, why don't you believe Him? (John 8:46)

Why do you worry? (Matt. 6:25–27)

What happens if you gain the whole world but lose your life? (Luke 9:25)

Use God-tracing.

These questions lead to God-tracing. As we seek to translate Jesus, we are learning to pay attention to people's stories so we can see God at work. First, Jesus must matter to us. How has Jesus affected your life? Second, others are worth the work of learning to speak their language. Perhaps people aren't attracted to Jesus or don't think they need Him because, as Christians, we don't seem to need Him ourselves. I want to introduce people to the love of Jesus that is available to them and visible in me. This is the Good News I have heard and will tell. When we're in conversation with someone about Jesus, it will be up to them to respond to it. Disciples of Jesus have the best news in their possession, and Jesus changes everything for all humankind.

This is still called evangelism. The Greek word is *euangelizō*, meaning "to bring good news."[4] Here's what evangelism is *not*:

- Making converts.
- Brainwashing.
- Forcing someone to believe.
- Telling people where they will go when they die if they don't believe in Jesus.

William Fay, well known for his classic *Share Jesus without Fear*, is known to have said, "There are only two motives for evangelism. Love of God and love of people. . . . Does your neighbor know the faith that is in you?"[5] If you want people to know Jesus, you must be open for them to know you. As they learn about you, let them hear stories about God. Everyone can trace everything back to Creator God, Father God, Omnipresent God. Let people wonder but not wander.

I listened one day as three young friends described their new experience of authentic Christian community in an anti-Christian city and how they had more joy than ever before. They said it all still seemed too good to be true. I asked if they were choosing to believe Jesus was the Only Way and the One responsible for their experience.

They replied, "He's too restrictive. He doesn't have an open-door policy, letting everyone into heaven. He doesn't cure everyone of cancer. People die young or are placed in abusive families. Parts of the world don't have clean drinking water. What is God doing about all of that?"

This is hard to wrap our minds around, but Christ did *something* two thousand years ago by coming to earth to live among us and show us very practically, yet supernaturally, how to overcome the world, care for the stranger, find healing and peace, and be loved unconditionally. Humanity has the resources to end some major global problems. We also live in a fallen world. My best response is, "I don't know what you're still searching for, but Jesus is here. You can choose to love Him back. I can attest I've seen Him. Hopefully you've seen something in me that has you curious."

Even with my three young friends' complaints about God, they are witnessing His love and His church. Society is witness to the benefits of some kingdom living, and rightly so if His disciples are in the world loving one another.

When you engage with someone, determine one thing you have in common. Perhaps you're both on the same flight. Perhaps you work for the same company. Or you live in the same town. You have kids at the same school. Let's take the example of your job as your commonality with this person. You can ask, "How did you get the job? Where did you get your gifts, talents, and education?"

Helping others trace their gifts, privileges, and very lives back to God gets them thinking outside of themselves.

My friends Pratyush and Gwen say that Christianity is not attractive to their colleagues and friends, yet these folks are very curious about how it works in their lives and why they've chosen this path. They speak of Jesus's teachings, which they practice, as a way to God-trace. Seek first His kingdom. Serve one another. Do not forsake gathering together. All of this is odd to their colleagues when they could be spending more time working, achieving goals, and making more money.

What good thing do you have that didn't come from God? Keep tracing it back, and you'll see everything begins with Him. "I say to the LORD, 'You are my Lord; I have no good apart from you,'" writes the psalmist (Ps. 16:2). Even if others can't see the connection, you can. So tell your story.

Don't we want Him to be in control, to rule in power? Think about His teachings, His justice, His mercy. Imagine your life where He's the one you answer to. Yes, this is submission—something we do all the time. We submit to street signs, airport protocol, shopping lines, and work guidelines.

If we make something or someone else our lord, our savior, our protection, Psalm 16:4 says, "the sorrows of those who run after another god shall multiply." Our happiness and well-being are attached to who or what we follow and adore.

If I want Jesus to be Lord of my life, what does that entail? I choose God. I then bless God. I set Him before me always. "Therefore my heart is glad, and my whole being rejoices. . . . You make known to me the path of life; in your presence there is fullness of joy; at your right hand are pleasures forevermore" (vv. 9, 11).

If your response is, "No thanks. I'm good. I don't need that," I'm more scared for you than you are of your invisible reality.

There is no "better than" syndrome in translating Jesus. There's "I want better for" syndrome though. I want better for me. Better for you. Better for our minds, thoughts, creativity, relationships, time, and margin. "I want better for you"—that's what a follower wants to say. As I seek better for my life, I do so through the person of Jesus.

Love Jesus back.

Matthew could think of no more reason to live. He had a plan to end his life and was moments away from making the jump. But a forceful hand grabbed his arm and pulled him back, and he lay on the ground in pain from his reality and from the landing. He was still alive. Who'd saved him? Where did that other person go? Matthew saw no one. He sought a different direction, believing that, for no other reason, he was not to try to take his own life ever again. Through Alcoholics Anonymous, Matthew was exposed to the teachings of Jesus. Later, he found our church. He tried the Alpha Course. For our retreat day, we met off-site. Matthew had not given thought about the location until he arrived. He had not been to this place in three years. Our Alpha retreat was a stone's throw from his attempted suicide spot. Matthew saw again how much Jesus loves him, and he couldn't help but love Him back.

Friend, if there is nothing else that stirs you in this book, let it be this: Jesus has done so much for you. Spend the rest of your living days loving Him back. In how you worship. In how you speak. In how you drive, cook, clean, and create. Love Jesus back as you work, play, give, and thrive. Love Jesus as you suffer, hurt, doubt, and pray. Love is a choice on our best and worst days. *I choose to love You, Jesus.* We love because He first loved us (1 John 4:19).

What's fascinating is how God takes the love you have for Him and taps a friend or two on the shoulder and points them to you. They see the love you have for Jesus. It stands out because they don't have it inside them yet.

What is the message the world needs to know to believe? Jesus loves them. We all get to love Jesus back. Culture can witness this in our stories and as we love one another.

God is not traced back to a building. He is found in His people. Jesus doesn't live inside your church. He's not curled up on the front row waiting until someone comes back the following day. He's not Flat Jesus in bookmark form holding your place in your Bible. We would never admit we've got Jesus in a box, but in our minds and our beliefs, where is He?

We put our faith in science, medicine, gravity, people, machines. We believe it will work when we turn it on. We believe it will hold us up when we sit on it. We believe the mechanic will fix what's broken. We believe the sun will melt the snow. Much of this we can't see. We see only the effects, not their origin.

Come to the end of yourself, and then you'll find Jesus. If you haven't needed Him yet, you're still doing it all on your own. You must be tired.

It's hard to get my mind around both questions. How can God love us this much? How can the world not love Him back? We watch the news and feel baffled, wondering why anyone upon hearing the warnings would not evacuate. The storm passes and we're shaking our heads, saddened at lost lives. Why didn't they leave when they had the chance?

Jesus is our rescue. He loves us so much He sacrificed Himself to make us a way out of selfishness, addiction, pride, depression, trauma. Receive His love. Love Him back. That's the Good News. The gospel. God loves you (by giving Jesus in your place), so love Him back (by believing in Him as you turn from your way).

Prompting.

Jesus doesn't always make sense. Aren't some of the best things in life hard to explain?

THE TABLE

ALL PEOPLE WILL KNOW THAT YOU ARE MY DISCIPLES, IF YOU HAVE LOVE FOR ONE ANOTHER.

John 13:35

I told Monty and his mom to come over with their homemade olive loaf and we would serve plenty of vegetables with a side of meat, the reverse of how we typically cook in our home, but tonight would be special. They parked by the curb near the intersection where Lee's car accident had happened a few months ago. Monty had shared his story with us of coming to Christ. Now his mom needed direction and help in understanding this new way of life her son had found. We listened to her concerns. It was refreshing to be jolted from Christianese and to explain salvation and baptism and being a follower of Jesus in simple, clear words. To share that church is the family of God and we are still humans who mess up and need forgiveness and grace, and not just from other Christians either.

I'm certain we were all nervous about having dinner together in our home. For our own sakes, we wanted to get it right. Love was tangibly present. The source of such love was Jesus Himself. We could all attest that what we experienced at the table with one another wasn't just nice feelings from having a reunion of sorts or a by-product of eating good food. It was love. That very love brought Monty and his mom to our church for the first time while we were required to gather outdoors during the pandemic. When we could gather indoors, Monty wanted to be baptized. Though he is adopted by two moms who are some of the most caring parents I've ever met, it was special for Ben to baptize him on Father's Day.

We bless each of them. We speak good of one another. We see each other around the gate and intentionally meet up for coffee and lunch at the table. Monty walks the well-worn path as he continues to share his faith with everyone. He translates Jesus to his friends and his moms and his brothers.

This isn't just Monty's story. It's also both of his moms' stories, because his faith and decisions affect them. Our hearts and minds are open to learn and listen and love. And there is nowhere else we'd rather be.

15 Become Bilingual

God is in control of the languages of this world. Language is communication with one another, yet when God is in the midst of our communication, *communion* takes place—the exchange is deeper, more intimate. Languages are to serve God. The prophet Daniel said, "And to [God] was given dominion and glory and a kingdom, that all peoples, nations, and languages should serve him" (Dan. 7:14). The idea of one common language was taken away from humankind at the tower of Babel and given back at Pentecost. Here's what happened. Jesus observed Passover with His followers and was crucified the next morning. He was resurrected on the third day and had many encounters with His followers. Forty days after His resurrection, Jesus returned to His Father in heaven. Ten days after that, God boldly sent His Holy Spirit upon His people in Jerusalem. This day was known as the Feast of Harvest, and Christians today refer to it as Pentecost, which means *fifty* in Greek. God poured out His Spirit that we might proclaim Jesus to the nations in our languages. The Spirit speaks to us and gives us the words to say.

The book of Acts begins with mystical phenomena—it's like a scene from a movie, with tongues of fire and the miraculous ability to understand each other. Today, His Spirit can speak through any language, any people group, any dialect, any culture. Our language, the language of Christ, can be traced back to Pentecost. It was at this place the Holy Spirit was given to His people to make the best news ever accessible and clear to everyone: Christ died and was resurrected to free us from sin and death. That is the gospel. And it can be spoken in the language of culture. He has given us one Spirit, one faith, one hope, one love.

Becoming bilingual is the practice of proclaiming Christ among our people in a language they can understand. God is bringing us back to Himself so we can understand one another with Christ as the center of our lives. Matthew 26:73 tells us we develop a dialect when we become bilingual, "for your accent gives you away." So how do we become bilingual? Bring Jesus to others. Let love lead. Recline at the table.

Bring Jesus to others.

A college student approached me about an ongoing conversation she was having with her friend John. "I have a friend who wants to be a Christian," she said. "He was raised by Christian parents but didn't want anything to do with it, and now that he's in his twenties, he wants to come back to God." She told me that she'd shared her faith story of being a new Christian for about a year and invited John to come to church with her. "Now what?" she asked.

They met at the gate. He wanted access to the cross. She spoke culture. She spoke Christ. The best thing she did was share her story! Together, she and I prayed for John. I gave her three sentences to share with him: Jesus loves you, John. Love Him back by giving Him your whole heart. Love others by following Jesus for the rest of your life.

"Okay. I'll give that a try," she said.

This doesn't make sense to the outside world. What we read in the Bible—the stories, the promises, the truths—has to be translated to our people. Jesus didn't distribute tracts or wear a "What Would Jesus Do?" bracelet or salvation beads. These things may translate in our Christian context, but that doesn't mean they'll translate to our local context. Jesus told Matthew, "Follow me" (Luke 5:27). Jesus told the woman caught in adultery "Go, and from now on sin no more" (John 8:11). He told the woman with the blood issue, "Your faith has made you well" (Matt. 9:22). With Saul of Tarsus, Jesus blinded him with a question: "Saul, Saul, why do you persecute me?" (Acts 9:4 NIV). Jesus spoke their language.

To speak the language of Christ to this culture is to speak the language of love. To speak the language of culture is to look for opportunities to give Christ's love. For without love, we are out-of-sync, noisy instruments (1 Cor. 13:1). This college student led with love as she shared her personal story of following Jesus in order to connect with John. She got Jesus and her friend occupying the same place.

This is all straight from Scripture—a theology that is super basic and supernatural. Jesus told us to multiply, to go and make disciples. To do this as His disciples, we bring Jesus with us to others who don't believe yet. Disciples are crucified with Christ, and we no longer live, but He lives in us (Gal. 2:20). This mystery of Christ-in-us means we are actually the body of Christ (Col. 1:27; 1 Cor. 12:27). We are each in Him as a new creation (2 Cor. 5:17).

Disciples don't have to search this world for peace, love, joy, hope, faith, or healing. If we are in Christ, we are in peace, love, joy, hope, faith, and healing. Feeling the presence and absence of these things is the normal ebb and flow of the spiritual life. If its absence is brought about by our wrongdoings, we repent.

This is what followers of the Way have coined as the Great Commission, when Jesus left Planet Earth into our care. His last words were for us to go and make disciples and that God would stay with us in Spirit form (Matt. 28:20). He is in us. When we show up, He is there. Fellow disciples, we need Jesus in us to translate Him. He has the words of life. He is what our world needs, which means we have what this world needs. Stop worrying about how to talk about Jesus. Love people with the words of living water. Let it flow through you and out of you. The results—how people respond—are not on you. Our friends and family will more likely consider Jesus on a personal level if we talk about Him like He's personal to us. Get Him flowing out of you by telling your story, encouraging someone with His words, and praying with them. You have Jesus. You have the language. The Holy Spirit will give you the words to say.

George MacDonald used fairy tales to tell stories, and it got C. S. Lewis's attention. MacDonald wrote in an essay, "The best thing you can do for your fellow, next to rousing his conscience, is not to give him things to think about, but to wake things up that are in him; or say, to make him think things for himself."[1]

Do you believe Jesus came to you? Then exercise that same faith in believing Jesus can come to them. Do you believe Jesus loves them? Then act with that same love so they feel it for themselves. Do you believe there's hope for this life? Then do not hoard it for yourself, for I've got a strong, urgent sense He's got enough hope for us all. When you pay attention to who you are around and who is active inside of you, a participation begins. "We start by loving them for Him and we soon love them for themselves," wrote Dorothy Day.[2]

Becoming bilingual requires faith—faith that God is still using people like us to give His message of hope and love. Faith that God is working in people's lives, revealing Himself, softening hearts, using circumstances, orchestrating you and me to be here and there with Him in His work.

When we are aware we bring Jesus into the presence of people, a joy wells in us that is satisfying. You are a bilingual follower and disciple of the living Lord! Truthfully, while you bring Jesus to them, in a mystical way Jesus is also there to welcome *you*. Strange how this happens.

Let love lead.

You are not the first to share your faith with someone, and what can feel terrifying can save someone's life. The cause might have seemed lost that day at the Lion's Gate with Stephen's blood on the ground. However, the Good News continued to be translated and went across borders and boundaries in exponential ways. What typically happens when something gets passed down? Over time it loses its punch, power, and pizzazz. But what if it was documented? Practiced? Respected? Kept sacred? What if something that happened back then is still alive and active in His followers right now? "Love had become in the disciples a 'holy must,'" wrote Eberhard Arnold.[3] Can you say, "I love you too much to not share Jesus" to those you meet?

Love can lead and not be received. Love can be expressed by one and repressed by the other. My friend Dani had a lovely twenty-minute conversation with a barista, as no one else was in line. Because this barista was open to Dani, she reached in her bag and tried to give her an Easter church invite card. Everything changed. The barista refused the invite, waving her hands. She was open to Dani, but then Jesus became more visible. Jesus taught His disciples—us—that when people listen to us they are listening to Him, and when people reject us they are rejecting Him. Because Jesus lives in us, the rejection feels personal. It is personal. But as disciples who have gone before us demonstrate, don't hold it against them.

We don't love in order to convert. We love because we've encountered Jesus. He is changing our lives, and it would be a hate crime to keep love from others.

I'd answer your call in the middle of the night.

I'd host you in our home if you were fleeing your home country.

I'd get you to a doctor if you were sick.

I'd buy you food if you had none.

I'd come and sit with you if you were grieving.

You must understand I'd also introduce you to Jesus if you haven't met Him or have run from Him.

Britton swapped this story with me on a Sunday: a lady on the bus on his route to church was asking for money for food. Someone she approached said, "Come with me to church. They're serving breakfast this morning." She refused the invitation and then approached Britton. He kindly told her, "You were just given an invitation, an answer to your need." He encouraged her to reconsider the offer.

Not everyone you share the love of Jesus with believes Jesus can love them. You translate Jesus and let Him transform them. Jesus is so good to invite us to receive His love and give it away. This is when prayer proves powerful. Take that very love you lead with and pray for that woman on the bus.

Jesus, the one You love is hungry and just turned down a perfectly good invitation. She must not understand. We're doing our part here on the bus. Come and get her attention like You did for me.

Pray this prayer for that barista:

Jesus, the one You love serves coffee but has a hard time receiving. I tried for the both of us, and we were just rejected. Don't give up on her just like You didn't give up on me. Pry her heart open, because she'll only be more amazing with Your love in her.

We learn this prayer language from Mary, who sent word to Jesus concerning her sick brother, Lazarus: "the one you love is sick" (John 11:3 NIV). As love leads, your prayers change and your noun is now plural, being you and Jesus.

The one *we* love, Jesus, is sick.

The one *we* love, Jesus, is in prison.

The one *we* love, Jesus, is looking to everything else.

The one *we* love, Jesus, is anxious.

The one *we* love, Jesus, has stepped away from her faith.

The one *we* love, Jesus, wants nothing to do with me or you.

But is it worth all of this—to take our beliefs of Jesus and practice them only to be met with criticism? Why not just keep quiet in this anti-Christian culture where people don't want to be bothered by our Christian views anyway? Besides, our Christian circles and churches are safe places to openly and comfortably talk about our faith.

If Jesus isn't at work in you, then you live a life without conviction. The sooner you stop acting surprised that the lost act lost, the sooner you'll be able to recline at the table just like Jesus.

Also, while we're all uncomfortable, let's note that comfortable Christianity doesn't exist. To be Christian is to follow Jesus in obedience. Most of His commands and teachings require us to be present in a hostile culture. If your Christian life is comfortable, you've strayed from your faith. The table will be confrontational and might be controversial. This is why we want to borrow Jesus's confidence and certainty. He will be a calm and curious presence that helps our winsome witness.

Recline at the table.

Jesus knew the cross was ahead of Him, but so was the resurrection. We know suffering is ahead of us, but so is His resurrection power. Because of this truth, we can relax even at a table with conflict. Confidence and certainty grow in His presence. They grow around the table. The more you tell your story of Jesus, the more your faith grows. The more you pay attention to culture prayerfully, the more your love grows.

Eight thousand people in San Francisco identify as homeless.[4] Even that number is off, as some are truly without a home and others are addicts living on the streets. When I moved to San Francisco, I was afraid of everyone living on the streets. I didn't know them or what they wanted. Over time, I began to make eye contact and see each person as made in the image of God. If I get afraid these days, it's out of fear of what is controlling them. I borrow Christ's confidence and certainty that He who began a good work in me has a good work for every homeless person and addict in my city. I love them. I pray for them. I speak with dignity to them.

The world doesn't have to be told we've been with Jesus today, but the world will know we've been with Jesus. In His short time physically on earth, Jesus often told individuals not to tell about Him, but in their not-telling, they told! Some of us try to translate Jesus before He's finished a particular work in us, or we intercept a teachable moment with Him to sculpt a post to the world—to start our tower building—instead of staying at the table, sharing with a few.

Jesus loved tables. He loved to have conversation around them and wasn't selective about who was gathered. While there are many cultural differences between the first century and the twenty-first century, tables continue to symbolize friendship and intimacy.

Culturally, the people of Jesus's time and place ate like the Greeks, who reclined horizontally with a hand propping up the head to eat at mealtime.[5] Now that's reclining! Before I knew this, I pictured Jesus leaning back in His chair, shoulders relaxed, smiling every time someone else came in. This is how we recline at the table. Be confident and certain that Jesus wants this more than you. How does reclining have anything to do with translating Jesus? Trust Jesus with your life and the people in your life. If you can recline, you are trusting. If you're trusting, reclining will be your posture.

I like to think the phrase "the more the merrier" was a Jesus original. Jesus was always making room at the table. He never worried what people thought of Him. He knew who He was and to whom He belonged. This makes a big difference as we become bilingual. We can live with Christ's confidence and certainty in who we are as His followers.

Imagine the influence you can have if you live this way. Live certain that Jesus is who He claims to be, did what He set out to do, and loves every single person around you. Live confident that His Spirit lives in you, is actively making you more like Him, and is visible to others around you.

Jesus also knew that His love was for everyone, but not everyone wanted His love. We can still be confident and certain inside this reality. People will be more drawn to His love in us when we are confident of His love in us. Our stories will be more believable when we share with certainty that our lives have been changed.

He demonstrated what He taught—He came to call sinners, not the righteous (Mark 2:15–17). I heard a message from my pastor that Jesus didn't come for the self-righteous but for the needy. Why? The self-righteous think they can save themselves and don't need a Savior. It's the needy who make room and have room for Him.

Jesus meets us where we are but doesn't leave us as we are.[6] This is a beautiful distinction of Christianity. Disciples are to always be learning, growing, changing, and becoming more like Him. People followed Him all over the country, but the place the Gospel writers describe Him as being most relaxed was when He was "reclining at table."

When Jesus was at the table, he was always reclining, except the time he needed to turn some tables over. He had a nonanxious presence among his culture.[7] Those around the table with Him were diverse. They didn't determine His beliefs of who He was or what He could do. He reclined with confidence and certainty. Why did He eat with tax collectors and sinners? (Are you eating at the table with tax collectors and sinners?) Tax collectors and sinners were in separate categories, because culturally tax collectors were seen as worse than sinners. That's pretty bad. They were categorically known to rob from the poor to benefit the rich and powerful.

Why was Jesus so comfortable around a table with such people? I get nervous each week at the start of Alpha, because this is where my friends see a clear picture of what I really believe and are given opportunities to decide if they believe in Jesus. Truth is, I can recline. I can relax. None of this is up in the air. It's already complete. Victory, salvation, resurrection—it's taken care of. I can relax my shoulders and smile. I've made my decision. I have decided to follow Jesus, no turning back. The cross before me. The world behind me.[8]

Christ is approachable. Are you? He is welcoming. Are you? He is winsome. Are you? He can recline because He has all authority in heaven and earth, and He is telling the truth. We can recline at the table because He's given us His authority as we share His truth.

Jesus sat down with people. He attracted diverse crowds. People could come to Jesus when they weren't received in the synagogue, in their hometowns, by their families or communities. He was attractive. People then made a decision to pursue or pass.

Jesus went into people's homes. Jesus enjoyed meals with people. He invited Himself over. He went where He was welcomed. Then there was that time He was asked to leave a place.

More on this in chapter 17. Jesus went, but He left His Spirit with the man because we bring Jesus to people!

Put it together.

The language of love is universal through the power of the Holy Spirit because of the cross of Christ. Your love for me will get my attention.

16 Know the Landscape

It can take months or years for a friend of mine to give church a try. This time, however, it was the easiest invite ever.

Jennifer was afraid to die, so she reached out to her one Christian friend, who lived in another country. This friend suggested she find a local church running the Alpha Course. Jennifer found our church online and emailed me, and we planned to meet between our services in the lobby. This was a brand-new experience for her, and as she shared her story with me, I grew more stunned that she showed up in the first place.

"What's all going on around here?" she asked. I began to point out our greeters, our kids' team, students meeting together, the coffee bar, all while thinking *I'm pointing out family.* I was in wonder of the smiles and laughter and joy Jennifer was seeing too.

"Where's that singing coming from?"

Our second service had begun. She was hearing worship music. She was hearing people sing to Jesus.

"Can we go in?"

"Of course!"

"Can I call my fiancé who dropped me off? He's probably in his pajamas still."

"Pajamas are fine, but whatever he wants to do."

I'd probably say that differently next time, but whatever. This was real and raw and now.

I gave her space to call her fiancé. I grabbed Mark and Sally, a young married couple who were small group leaders, and introduced them to Jennifer while we waited for Ross, her fiancé, to show up.

We found a few seats in the back of the auditorium, and that day I experienced church through Jennifer and Ross. The more I listened to the message, songs, and announcements about being part of a family and coming home, the more I wondered if this sounded cultish to them. I prayed they were feeling loved and welcomed and could see straight inside of us as real people who loved Jesus.

The service finished, and they stayed for our next steps lunch, met the pastors, made a few new friends, and signed up for Alpha.

"See you next Sunday," they said.

And we did.

We are to live transformed lives. Jesus set it up so our lives would be attractive to the fearful living among us, calling them toward hope. "As theologian and archbishop Rowan Williams notes, 'The Church is essentially missionary and has the capacity to attract others to this pilgrim community of faith as it passes through this world.'"[1] So how do we get the people on our minds and in our lives and Jesus in the same place? I hope as we are at the table now, we give this question its much needed weight and consideration.

The people on my mind as I write this book are culturally relevant but spiritually shy. I see other readers who are spiritually mature yet culturally frustrated. I think of the Nones[2] who have given up on the church of Jesus Christ and are finding culture to be a spiritual place to find community. I see friends in my Alpha group who are figuring out how to believe in Jesus and engage in society. I see missional Christians who are aware of the lost in their towns but are at a loss on how to reach them.

Translating Jesus is a shared experience that is less scripted and more Spirit-filled. Everyone involved is mindfully present that something big is taking place here, and this, my friends, is the kingdom of God, the landscape at the table.

Expect an experience.

Someone gave Ben and me a gift card to a restaurant we knew little about, Al's Place in the Mission. As our holiday trip had been canceled, we made a date night of it. We planned to simply go to the restaurant and use our gift card. But when we arrived, we saw a line had formed outside. We discovered there were only two seatings for the evening. We would all start our meals about the same time. This was more exquisite than we thought. After we were seated and greeted and given glasses of water, we watched as the staff moved around the small corner restaurant with graceful synchronization. Every worker was doing every job. They knew everything. Ben and I took a look at the menu. It was one of those where we could recognize only a word or two in the description of an item. This would take time. Or it wouldn't. We were easily convinced to go with the chef's *pre fixe* menu. By faith we put our next few hours in his hands. In the soup we tasted hints of mushroom, pomegranate, and nuts. We asked what was in it. The server said it had sixty-two ingredients. How can you even get that many items in a bowl? When the colorful salad was delivered, we were told the chef preferred we eat it with our hands. We didn't want to disappoint the chef. Every item brought to our table wowed us. We finished our time at the restaurant by doing something we've never done before or since. We got permission to go back to the kitchen and personally thank the chef and his staff.

After that experience at Al's Place, we wanted to plan our next date. Try new menus. Tell others about it. Now, I can tell you about Al's. You can believe what I say about Al's. But not until you experience it for yourself do you *know*. Experience is knowledge. I don't just believe it's good; I've experienced its goodness.

We want our friends to experience Jesus—to have an encounter with the living Christ. Our friends can't just believe. They must accept Jesus. Getting them to believe isn't enough. Not until they experience will they *know*. Our friends can experience Jesus with us as we bring Christ into conversation and daily practices such as prayer, implementing His teachings in our decisions, and letting the fruit of the Spirit be visible. Al's Place was good, but it was even better because I wasn't alone in the experience.

Enjoy Spirit-filled fellowship.

Not everyone is a fan of the church. This is a sad truth. Jesus is the head of the church and has entrusted the church into the hands of His followers. This is a sobering truth.

Many see the church as a building, a physical place, a Christian house of worship. How do you see the church? The church Saul persecuted was a collection of Christians. They were always gathering, meeting needs. It was persecution that scattered them every single time.

Jesus is not just the head of the church but also the host of the table. Jesus first mentioned "church" when He said He would build His church and the gates of hell would not prevail against it (Matt. 16:17–19). He established the church at Pentecost as people translated Jesus to others, and this led to thousands being added to this fellowship. This is how the church grows and spreads.

Inyoung grew up attending church in Korea. In her adult years, she'd sneak in and then disappear after the service, avoiding all forms of engagement and fellowship. Her goal was to get a sprinkle of God in hopes it would appease Him and get her by. Inyoung moved for her job, and in her new home she tried sneaking into another church. Then, although she knew it would cost her, she made a decision to get involved in a small group. This led to new friendships and a hunger to be with that faith community on a regular basis. People knew her, and this started to matter. The time she spends in this fellowship comes back to her in abundance during the week.

We are physical and spiritual beings. God made us. Then God breathed His life into us (Gen. 2:7). "It is the spirit in a person, the breath of the Almighty, that gives them understanding," says Job 32:8 (NIV). The Spirit of the living God longs to be activated in us. As Christ followers, we get to give people an experience of God's love through us. We get to invite people to church and into Christian fellowship where they can feel His conviction and

His kind mercy through music, the teaching of God's Word, and community. Then this happens:

> The Spirit, not content to flit around on the surface, dives into the depths of God, and brings out what God planned all along. Who ever knows what you're thinking and planning except you yourself? The same with God—except that he not only knows what he's thinking, but he lets us in on it. God offers a full report on the gifts of life and salvation that he is giving us. We don't have to rely on the world's guesses and opinions. We didn't learn this by reading books or going to school; we learned it from God, who taught us person-to-person through Jesus, and we're passing it on to you in the same firsthand, personal way. (1 Cor. 2:10–13 Message)

We often don't think about taking up residency on the planet as much as we think about moving around town each day. You can be in your bedroom inside your house. You can be inside a store inside a mall. There is your body and there is your spirit inside of your body. You think about your body, but do you think about your spirit? Imagine: If the Holy Spirit got attention in your body, how much more would you be alive?

People need to see Spirit-filled Christians, a Spirit-filled collection of Christ followers. We are a gift to the people and a presence in our culture. The kingdom of God is all around us. To translate Jesus, we have to enter the kingdom and step outside of the church. My friend Gwen could not do all of God's commands in Singapore because the naked, homeless, and prisoners weren't visible or accessible. Then she moved to San Francisco. As she led one of the city's largest egg hunts as our church outreach, she dialogued with one of her volunteers and discovered he was homeless. He was delighted to serve because it filled him with memories of Easter with his kids.

Alister McGrath writes that the church is called to proclaim Christ, not preach about walls and fences. He goes on to say, "We are called upon to know both the Christian faith and the wider culture that lies beyond the walls of the church, with a view to bringing these into conversation."[3]

We need to be around people whom we don't pick as our inner circle, people different from us, people who are in different seasons than we are. We can still have our affinity groups during the week, but we need to be a part of the church of Jesus Christ in a local context in person on a weekly basis.

Do you have a membership at a gym, grocery warehouse, or vacation club? Do you have social media accounts? Membership gives us access and say-so.

A Harvard Divinity School fellow observed this about Peloton, an American exercise company with monthly subscribers:

Peloton is part of a much bigger trend he calls "unbundling." Within that, people are now browsing in a variety of places for things they once got all at a congregation: worship, scripture, life transitions and social justice among them.[4]

His observations point out the irony that these memberships create a cultlike following, though participants shun organized religion for being such. Community is a bad god but a wonderful companion. Some are in the habit of cherishing community through podcasts, posts, and preachers at the expense of a Spirit-filled fellowship with other believers and an intimate relationship with Christ Himself.

Do you need to believe in the church again? This is the place designated for you to get training, prayer, wisdom, and encouragement to go out and practice the language of Christ during the week. John Stott concurs, "Every Christian needs to belong to a local church and share in its worship, fellowship, and witness."[5] Jesus ought to be magnified and lifted up above anything and everything else at your local church. If not, join another company elsewhere. His kingdom is growing and impacting this world, and there's no time for so-called church politics, platforms, or power pastors. His kingdom is being filled with Christians who are attached to local churches and serving and reaching their local contexts.

Enter the kingdom.

Imagine a friend tells you he's throwing a party and needs your help: "I sent out the invites and people sent their regrets. I've heard every excuse you can think of. They have no idea what they're missing out on."

"How can I help?"

"I'm so glad you asked!" Your friend's face brightens. "I'm hosting this party no matter what, and I want my house full. Will you go and invite whoever you see? I'm not picky at all. I will turn no one away. They don't need to bring anything, though they are welcome to bring anyone. All they have to do is come."[6]

This is the kingdom table. We bring laughter, family, and joy because we're all connected anyway! What joy is on the other side of becoming bilingual? Seeing people experience Jesus.

As you disciple others, help them depend on the Holy Spirit for growth. We all have tools and resources that help our spiritual growth, but the Holy Spirit is our best guide. Help them listen and learn from the Spirit, as you do.

What we experience in Spirit-filled fellowship in the presence of Christians and non-Christians is otherworldly. Can you think of an experience you had that was beyond normal, beyond your limited human expectation? I can think of a day we had with our friends in Tuscany that we call "Best Day Ever," because it was filled with one surprise after another. I think of a time we treated a special friend to a day in Napa. I think of standing at a train station and receiving the most incredible news via email. I think of hundreds of us prayer walking downtown San Francisco asking God to give us a permanent church home. This is love. This is the work of the Holy Spirit in our lives.

Set the table, and Jesus will take over (Luke 24:28–30). The fellows walking to Emmaus invited Jesus to be their guest, but it was He who took the bread and broke it. Then they knew Him! What is possible at the bilingual table when you acknowledge Jesus is part of the experience? He loves tables.

Live in such a way that the kingdom of God is here and now. That's how God designed it. Religious people are still asking when the kingdom of God will come, as if they want to get this life over with and move on to a rewarding, exclusive club in heaven. Jesus taught us His kingdom is not a place we can point to but a present reality we can experience (17:20–21). Every Christian is heir to His kingdom that is here on earth (Rom. 8:17). We pray for His kingdom, His rule to come on earth as it is in heaven. We speak with confidence of whom we belong to, of what we believe, and of why we love one another.

We don't build the kingdom of God; we enter it, for it's already established.

Put it together.

You know you're at the table when you find yourself needing to speak both languages.

17 Live with Your People

I imagine this was the last conversation between the wild and uncontrollable man of Mark 5 and Jesus before He got back into the boat:

Jesus: "They're asking Me to leave, not you. It works best this way. Your life has been radically changed. They know you, and you can help them know Me."

The man: "They think I'm still crazy. I've got no friends among them. You know what they're saying, and they're not entirely wrong. This is such a messy and confusing story, Jesus. I'm not so sure it will translate. I was a wild and uncontrollable man. You called me by name and restored me to my right mind. They were afraid of me then, and I think they are more afraid of me now. What do I even say?"

Jesus: "You've got our story now. Tell them how much the Lord has done for you, and how He has shown mercy on you."

The man: "You've set me free, and I thought that was impossible. If You're not here, how do You plan on freeing the townspeople from their fears? They are afraid; not to mention the pig herders who ended up with a very bad day."

Jesus: "Welcome the people. Live for them. Make friends with those who don't believe yet."

This man didn't have religious words. He'd spent years tormented by demons, exiled from his home and his community. Imagine what it was like for him to tell his Jesus story with his own people. If he can, we can.

Telling your people about the Good News doesn't mean you water it down. It's already accessible to every man and woman, boy and girl. Jesus often spoke to illiterate crowds in such a way they could grasp God's love for them.

I've heard Christians say, "If Jesus would just do this in people's lives here . . ." Well, Jesus demonstrates through this story that it will be our very lives, our story told in our voices, that He will use to amaze people. This man still had to live with people who didn't understand Jesus and were afraid of him. Interestingly, it's often us, His disciples, who are scared of sharing our faith stories when those we're telling them to are the scared ones. We believe the lie that it's better to just respect each other's views and not rock the boat. Safer. Instead, we need to practice obedience and do what Jesus tells us to do. As He said to this man, "Go home to your own people and tell them how much the Lord has done for you" (Mark 5:19 NIV).

Welcome the people.

It's easier to stick to the people who are like you, but if that hasn't gotten boring yet, give it time. Or you can encounter people the way Jesus does. People are holy ground. They are images of God. Let this significant and profound truth affect your soul. **This is**

the mindset of evangelism. We find Jesus in other human beings. When it's Christians among Christians, it's easier. When you're with atheists, agnostics, Nones, and others, you love them because you see with hope what Jesus can do in them. You share with people how wonderful, marvelous, and one-of-a-kind they are because of Jesus.

Notice what Matthew did after Jesus told him to follow Him. Luke documents that he had a party and invited all his sinner and tax collector friends. We don't call people by those labels today. We use other words. Former tax collector turned disciple Matthew left his job and his lifestyle but didn't leave his people. If Jesus could call him, Matthew knew Jesus could also call his kind of people. Matthew demonstrated a tangible truth for us: repentant people are receptive people. Matthew experienced Jesus by receiving His love and loving Him back as he left his deceptive and lucrative business. He instantly became free to welcome others. Paul wrote about this welcoming freedom in Romans 6: "But thank God you've started listening to a new master, one whose commands set you free to live openly in his freedom!" He went on to say, "I'm using this freedom language because it's easy to picture" (vv. 18–19 Message).

Consider Harriet Tubman's life again. She wanted more people to come and experience freedom, so she herself became their welcomer. Harriet welcomed Joe to freedom, and he wrote a song about it: "Glory to God and Jesus too, one more soul got safe; oh, go and carry the news, one more soul got safe."[1] As we become bilingual, we can replicate Tubman's back-and-forth life as she was a friend to strangers both free and enslaved, interceded for them, expected the Holy Spirit to show up, and ran in freedom only to do it all over again and again.

185

Paul also understood the life on the path between the gate, the cross, and the table. He went back to people he had been to before. Antioch—Iconium—Lystra—Derbe—Lystra—Iconium—Antioch. To do what? To keep on "strengthening the souls of the disciples, encouraging them to continue in the faith, and saying that through many tribulations we must enter the kingdom of God" (Acts 14:22).

At the cross, we experience freedom and run in the path of Jesus's commands at the gate, for He sets our hearts free to invite others to the table. For ages, we've tied Christianity to a religion and not a relationship. We can thank the Pharisees and Sadducees for this, but if they didn't do it, someone else would have. As disciples, we get to live out this freedom at the gate, the cross, and the table. Freedom and welcome are found in relationship, not religion. That's what Matthew experienced. That's what the wild and uncontrollable man and the townspeople who believed got to experience. It's what Harriet and Joe and many other enslaved people experienced. Paul did as well, for he wrote,

> What we've learned is this: God does not respond to what we do; we respond to what God does. We've finally figured it out. Our lives get in step with God and all others by letting him set the pace, not by proudly or anxiously trying to run the parade. (Rom. 3:27–28 Message)

This is the mindset of discipleship. To this day, Christianity is hard to explain and best understood lived. Imagine Matthew's table, full of people not welcomed by religious folks. In one day, Matthew went from not knowing Jesus, to following Jesus, to welcoming Jesus and others to his table. The table symbolizes doing life together, no matter how messy and ongoing the conversations may be. Let us keep the path well worn between the three places—gate, cross, and table—in which Christ and His followers spent their lives. "There is neither Jew nor Greek, there is neither slave nor free, there is no male and female, for you are all one in Christ Jesus" (Gal. 3:28). That's who we are. That's why we welcome.

Live for others.

We must learn to live for others. Not live for people's approval but for *them*, because that's what Jesus Christ does. See God and the world together, not separate. When Jesus died for all of us, He didn't do so to then distance Himself from us. He did so to come close. He died for us. He lives for us. He is always with us. Becoming bilingual is looking at Jesus and seeing others, looking at others and seeing Jesus. **This is the essence of reconciliation.** Look at these three expressions from Paul about Jesus.

To the Christians in Philippi, he wrote, "In humility count others more significant than yourselves. Let each of you look not only to his interests, but also to the interests of others" (Phil. 2:3–4).

To the Christians in Corinth, Paul wrote, "We regard no one from a worldly point of view. . . . All this is from God, who reconciled us to himself through Christ. . . . We are therefore Christ's ambassadors [coworkers, translators], as though God were making his appeal through us. . . . Be reconciled to God" (2 Cor. 5:16, 18, 20 NIV). In other words, Jesus loves you. Love Him back. Love one another.

To the Christians in Rome, Paul wrote, "Let each of us please his neighbor for his good, to build him up" (Rom. 15:2). This is what Christ did for us. "Therefore welcome one another as Christ has welcomed you, for the glory of God. . . . Christ became a servant . . . in order that the Gentiles might glorify God for his mercy" (vv. 7–9).

> So, my dear friends, don't take my rather bold and blunt language as criticism. . . . I'm simply underlining how very much I need your help in carrying this highly focused assignment God gave me, this priestly and gospel work of serving the spiritual needs of the non-Jewish outsiders so they can be presented as an acceptable offering to God, made whole and holy by God's Holy Spirit. (vv. 15–16 Message)

Paul was becoming bilingual and translating Jesus to bring His love to the places where Jesus was not yet known or worshiped.

By translating Jesus, we come to know one another. Leonardo Boff wrote,

> But it was by seeing, imitating, deciphering [translating], and living with Jesus that his disciples came to know God and the human person. The God who is revealed in and through Jesus is human. And the human being who emerges in and through Jesus is divine.[2]

Throw away the idea that caring for people who are far away from God is un-Christian.

One regular morning, I spent some time writing at a bakery. I initially didn't tip the worker, but after a time she went on break and sat down kitty-corner from me.

Give her the one-dollar bills in your wallet. That had to be the Holy Spirit, because it wasn't my natural thought.

I did so, and she and I began to talk. I shared Jesus while I was sharing about raising teenagers alongside my husband.

She returned to work shortly, and we both smiled, having enjoyed a brief encounter with a stranger. Another lady soon took her seat. She wore a cross necklace and pulled out Bible study materials from a tote bag. We conversed about the internet abruptly not working and what *was* working in our lives. I asked her who introduced her to Jesus. She told me of her brother, whose brother-in-law had died of cancer at thirty, and how this tragic death began a spiritual search for him and his wife. In their search, they found Christians and Christian community, and shared their learnings with their extended family. The family grew up nonpracticing Buddhists and now were first-generation Christians. This lady in the bakery now lives for Jesus and lives to tell others about Him.

God, give us a vision for others that is impossible without You.

How I care for people in San Francisco looks different than it would in San Diego, Brooklyn, Billings, or Gulf Breeze. Love your local people. We've got different dialects, and it matters how we speak to culture and listen to culture. We ought not compare one to the other.

All the letters Paul wrote are to local contexts, local cultures. Yes, we are more global than ever before, but to reach and care, we have to speak Christ and local culture.

Going to conferences can produce takeaways, resources that can be pulled out and applied to your context. Second Corinthians 10:13 tells us to boast in the Lord of stories with our giftings and influence, "so that we may preach the gospel in lands beyond you" (v. 16). But it starts by welcoming and living for the people right where we are.

At a Mediterranean restaurant downtown for date night, Ben and I prayed with our eyes open for every person at the restaurant we could set eyes on with this renewed reality: *these are our people, whom we are called to love and serve and lead.* Followship says wherever Jesus leads, we'll go. Leadership says living for others is our responsibility.

Keep close friendships with non-Christians.

Why should we keep close friendships with non-Christians? Because a day is coming when the presently closed door will become open, and we will say alongside disciple John Stott, "We have been strangers; now we are friends. There has been a closed door between us; now we are seated at the same table."[3]

Language is not all learned at church. Even the language of Christ gets practiced out in culture. People need to meet Christians who are churchgoers and culture learners. It's not enough to know non-Christians. We've got to be engaging regularly in their lives. They need us to point them to truth and hope. They need us to pray with them and walk alongside them in this life. They need to see how we mess up and still come back to our Father who loves us and has a plan for our lives.

And us? We need them to ask us questions that cause us to search the Scriptures. We need them to share with us their very lives to grow our very prayers and faith. We need non-Christian friendships because Christ's love is intended to flow out from us into them.

Non-believers matter so much to us and to Jesus. Jesus was in relationships with those who didn't believe in Him yet—how dare we ignore those who don't follow the Way yet? He kept Judas around all three years. Mary Magdalene was living a life of oppression when she and Jesus first met. Let us include everyone at the table, so everyone can meet Him.

First Corinthians 13:8 says, "Love never ends." Love doesn't stop with us or in us. We keep on loving. We don't have the option of quitting as Christ bearers. We might have enemies; we keep loving. People will leave the church, the city; we keep loving. We don't see the world or interpret Scripture the same; we keep loving. We let ourselves down and disappoint others; we keep loving.

A soft heart allows the Father to give us insights to this world that help us discern how to navigate the broken, difficult, and confusing thoughts, attitudes, and actions of the people around us. A soft heart toward our people gives space for the Holy Spirit to reveal His redemptive love. We keep each other close because we are made to be close—this human race God created. All of this is fascinating when you think about it.

One very interesting probability model created by a demographer for genealogists suggests that a child born in 1947 in England, tracing back to 1492, would have sixty thousand ancestors. Going back further, to 1215, this child would find 80 percent of the entire population of England at that time on his or her family tree![4]

Let's look at another model, found in Matthew 1. It's a long list of unfamiliar names known as the genealogy of Jesus Christ. For years, I skipped over this chapter. Why give attention to people

I don't know who don't mean anything to me? How wrong I've been.

Leave it up to Jesus to once again show us that it's not about being popular, influential, or knowing the right people for our stories to matter. This list is full of outsiders and outcasts, and all are a part of the lineage of Christ. Matthew also includes five women in this list of names at a time when women had no status. How wrong we are to think that no one knows or cares who we are.

We don't have to know how to pronounce their names or put faces to the names to know that every person listed in Matthew 1, the genealogy of Christ, matters a great deal. Honestly, our names wouldn't stand out to them either. But to the names before and after them, well, they mattered greatly. It was their grandfather who taught them their skill. It was their father who spoke truth and lived with integrity. It was their grandmother who abandoned a sinful cycle and surrendered to God and changed the course of her family. It was their mother who never took her eyes off God and always had a story of His faithfulness to share.

In a genealogy, someone brings someone into this world to influence, disciple, love, and care for them. In the genealogy of the Christian faith, someone introduced you to Christ because they loved you. We continue the genealogy by telling someone we love about Christ. Therefore we are all linked. We are all connected.

John led Andrew who led Peter to Jesus. Jesus called Peter and Paul. Paul called Timothy. Someone called you. And you must call someone else. To the people in the family of God, to those who introduced you to Jesus, who come alongside you, teach you, serve with you, you would say they matter greatly, right?

This is where all great stories start. At the beginning. In obscurity. I hope at the table you see the value of getting your story going, because your story matters. However, we have to be okay with not everyone knowing who we are. Only a few matter in this regard, and those are the ones whom God has put in our genealogies to influence and introduce us to His Son, Jesus Christ. God's heart is for us all to be reconciled to Him. Let us keep close to non-Christians friends, because we are strangers until we're not anymore.

Put it together.

It's easier to stick to people like you. Take the Christ challenge and make friends with someone different from you.

18   Swap Stories

Do you love a good story? Are you hopeful there will be more seasons and sequels? Do you ask friends what shows they are watching these days so you can add to your queue? I think our family lives a quite normal life until someone comments on our San Francisco stories, our adoption journey, or our RV chronicles. At times we have opened up our very lives because we think we're onto a good story.

On the third stop on our "Cruise Across America" RV adventure during the Christmas holidays, we had a sewage problem. When Ben and the boys were emptying the sewage tank, the hose busted. The little campground store didn't have any more. We'd have to wait until tomorrow, when we could get to a larger store. I had been documenting our journey, and this part was no exception. What wasn't always captured were the stressful conversations about whether we could successfully get to Georgia and back to California in this home on wheels. That was a sleepless night for me and Ben. We knew God cared for us but wondered if He had time for anything as silly as a sewage hose. Meanwhile, the kids were loving the adventure, the uncertain outcomes, and the false reality that they were in their parents' good hands.

The next morning, we were finishing up our breakfast when there was a knock on our RV door. Not typical. Not at a campsite three thousand miles from home. It's not like we were making friends in the community shower. We knew no one out here.

"Do we open the door?" It was that weird.

When we answered the door, the guy who'd knocked looked completely normal, but his question was supernatural: "I know this is odd, but do you guys need a sewage hose?"

Shea and his family were on a similar journey from Northern California to the East Coast. His pastor had been following our RV chronicles and reached out to him to see if by chance they were near our campsite. Shea stepped outside his camper and saw the sewage dilemma of his very next-door neighbor. We fit the description, and he thought he'd give it a brave try.

There are almost two hundred campsites at just one of the campgrounds in Albuquerque, New Mexico. Shea could have been miles ahead or behind us, but he was literally right next door that night. We discovered we both had plans to stay in Oklahoma the next night, and decided to intentionally stay at the same place this time, although God knew about the previous night.

As we shared our story, we heard from people across the country who knew Shea or his wife. God is a connecting God! He loves good stories. We shared s'mores and more stories that night in Oklahoma and laughed to think what God was setting up at campsites 61 and 62. While we were in a mess, God was navigating this family to the spot beside us. He set it up. Friend, if this doesn't have you putting your trust in Him and sharing your God story, I'll invite our friends back to tell you a little more of their ongoing stories.

Sundays are for swapping stories.

We need to let stories inspire us again. We consume our time with what I call flat stories—stories we only feel connected to in the moment, stories that don't enhance our lives. They are flatly displayed on a screen or a paper and are scrolled today and replaced tomorrow.

But what happens when we tell one another stories we're personally caught up in? Do we feel invited into something real? Is it true and meaningful and purposeful? I've chosen to tell you stories at the gate, the cross, and the table so you see the back-and-forth work of translating Jesus. You met Christine, Tiffany, and others in chapters 4 and 11, and as I share more here, keep in mind people tell stories that aren't finished yet. We share news that didn't go the way we had hoped. We bring up current events that bring up more questions. We swap stories, share news, and suggest ideas because we're invested.

The disciples had been invested in Jesus's life for three years. They were hiding and afraid when Jesus was arrested, their lives spiraling out of control. These disciples couldn't see the other side of the cross. They reacted differently to culture at the gate. The cross meant only death. When Jesus returned to His disciples after He returned to life, I imagine they swapped stories of when they first saw Him and how they were afraid and hid when He was arrested. They naturally put pieces together from each other's stories. These stories became the documents we call the Gospels, the Good News.

Christine and I met over coffee several times, shared countless text messages, had Zoom conversations, and engaged in book discussions of Francis Collins's *Language of God* and Josh McDowell's *More Than a Carpenter*.

"I've got nothing else to give you, Christine," I said one day. "I've told you all I know. You've consumed so much truth. You have to make this decision in faith—that's all there is to it."

A few weeks passed, and I reached out to Christine to see if she was coming to celebrate our friend Sheila's baptism. "You can bring your swimsuit if you want!" I told her, my way of saying she could be baptized as well.

When we greeted one another before Sheila's baptism, Christine whispered to me, "I've got my swimsuit on."

I gave her a look, wanting more.

"I'm ready to give my life to Jesus," she said, and smiled.

Sheila identified with Christ in baptism. Then Christine did. One story affected the other. As I baptized both friends in the days of a pandemic when no one could attend church, I could see all the faces of the people who prayed for Christine, served us countless magical cups of coffee, and authored books Christine read. I could see her family as well, those who believe and those who've yet to believe.

Tiffany, a few days after the Dandelion Chocolate intervention, made Jesus Lord of her life during a Sunday service and sent me this message:

What a day! I'm so excited that I took this decisive step in my faith journey. I feel a lightness that I haven't experienced. It's like I can breathe, literally. I can finally fill my lungs with air in a way that I haven't for some time now. This morning, I asked

God for that click to signify the moment. And soon I realized I could take deep breaths without any pain. It's been a while since I've been able to do this. Spiritually and physically I feel more alive now! I consider the responsibility that comes with being a Christian—it requires new attitudes, emotions, and practices. It's a gentle reminder, but daunting too. But I don't want the fear of "getting it right" to hold me back from receiving God's goodness as long as I work on being a good disciple.

As a fellow disciple, I can give my life to this! Tiffany's husband, Max, was baptized on the same day. They serve at church and are in community regularly.

Nikole, Nino, and Alli are tracing God as they open doors and create space for wonder. They believe God is at work around them, and He is bringing people and opportunities to them they can't make happen on their own. I'm here for it! Bilingual disciples see what culture longs to see as the cross reveals more of Jesus at the table. I recently had an email exchange with the girls. Nikole had asked me over chai, "How do you love Jesus back?" I had a better answer six months later as I read a verse in my morning time with Jesus. "What can I give back to the LORD for all the good things he has done for me? I'll lift up the cup of salvation. I'll call on the LORD's name" (Ps. 116:12–13 CEB). Here was my translation to these college girls:

How do you love Jesus back? David, the psalmist, says to celebrate the reality of what He's done for you and say yes to Jesus.

I share stories with you because this is how we translate Jesus to our world. When we experience Jesus ourselves and see His work in others, we tell it. Luke writes that on one occasion after

Christ's resurrection, Jesus was eating with His disciples. I presume at the table, since fast-food counter service wasn't a cultural thing. He gave them a grand mission: "Receive the Holy Spirit and be My witnesses everywhere you go" (see Acts 1:8). And then Jesus was gone. The disciples then worshiped, prayed, and read the Scriptures together. They had church. They received the Spirit, and then they dispersed to tell the story of Jesus with their whole lives. The God you worship corporately on Sundays longs to be introduced by you personally Monday through Saturday.

Mondays are for stepping into stories.

Since the Holy Spirit lives inside Christians, shouldn't He be easy to see? Sundays for sure, around a place like church, but what happens Monday through Saturday in we believers who have the Holy Spirit living inside of us? Many Christians receive Christ for salvation, but like most things in life, we get what we want out of it then move on with our agendas. We live only a halfhearted Christianity if we are living it for what we can get out of it. It's the power of the Holy Spirit unleashed in our lives that brings us completely and wholeheartedly to life.

Imagine if all you did was breathe in. Try it. Breathe in and do not exhale. It's impossible. We have to breathe out. We cannot tell our lungs to work. Only God can. That is spiritual energy. It's the Hebrew word *rûaḥ*.[1]

What do we do Monday through Saturday? *Rûaḥ*. Yes, we breathe in the Spirit and breathe out the Spirit—or we are breathing in flesh and breathing out flesh if we are not walking in the Spirit. Everyone who believes in Jesus receives the Holy Spirit. We know that, but do we know He will change us? I know it's scary to consider that the Spirit has set up shop inside us, and I get it. But He has people He wants us to see and encounters for each of us to step into.

Sunday gatherings fill us and bless us. Then comes Monday. Oh, the devil makes us feel as if we're all alone again.

God, we take back Mondays in Jesus's name. Let's go into this day together!

When we're at church on Sundays, we go into Mondays differently.

Jesus didn't tell the fishermen He'd make them accountants or lawyers or priests or cooks. He said He'd make them fishers of men, because that was their language. "Follow Me and I will make your vocation and calling eternal and relational for My kingdom" (see Matt. 4:18–20). Following Jesus is being fishers of men. If you reverse engineer this, then if you're not making disciples, are you even following Jesus? Show me who you are in conversation with each week, and I'll show you your Monday through Saturday priority and ministry.

Remember Dion the bus driver? Guess who took his bus twice a day for a school year? Our youngest son. That's a few of us praying over bus 44. Mondays are for stepping into stories, because connections happen among storytellers.

Connections happen among storytellers.

The lie we believe is that our story must be a viral, blockbuster, *New York Times* bestseller to have any shareable worth. However, the best stories are those that connect us and change us. Stories build if we let them—and if we let them out.

Fredrick Douglass wrote a letter explaining Harriet Tubman's private way of leading the cause and only getting a small thank-you compared to his way of leading the same cause in a public light.[2] Compare this to those who are called to translate Jesus on a stage or platform and those who have the conversations and relationships no one else sees.

If it weren't for a few people sharing their stories with me, I wouldn't know Jesus and be writing to you. If I hadn't told a few of my friends about Jesus, they'd still be in the despair and darkness they've told me about.

One Sunday I approached Fred and Claudine, my friends from Africa who consistently sit a few rows behind us at church. I asked how God had blessed them during the week. They shared how Claudine had a toothache for three weeks, and this week the pain was gone. Fred's boss had approached him, alongside fellow employees, and given him ample words of encouragement. Fred shared how he was moved to tears and overwhelmed. He made sure to point to heaven and share with his coworkers the source of his good work and who he works for. Fred and Claudine are people who frequently swap stories with me because of the stories they step into Monday through Saturday.

Jesus told His stories to believers and non-believers. It was often a mixed crowd. At the table, He could pull in His followers and the curious and admirers through storytelling. Jesus told stories that were translatable and teachable. Do you feel the gravity of what your story can do? I could talk about war-torn countries, pandemic aftermath, mass shootings, or social media and strike up a conversation with anyone. In my local context, I can talk about the school lottery system and the stress it brings, and also how we've found a whole new people group of families in the city who are open to the Christian values we practice at home. This is storytelling that is translatable and teachable. It's also practical. You tell stories that move people. Jesus can move their hearts. People can move their decisions.

Fred and Claudine were among a dozen or so others who reclined at our table one evening. As we finished up dessert, I asked, "What do you want to praise God for?" Fred shared a story of God healing a non-believing fellow employee's knee after he got to pray for him. Our young Egyptian friend Rany leaned in, amazed.

"How can you step into his story with such confidence?" he asked for all of us.

With such joy, Fred reminded us at the table we all have the same God, Christians and non-Christians. We're all connected.

"I just believe more than they do in the moment." Fred spoke with confidence.

Language and culture aren't barriers when the Holy Spirit is at work. Actually, nothing is a barrier. We're not expected to speak with polished speech! That takes the spotlight off the cross of Jesus Christ. As Paul wrote, "Christ did not send me to baptize, but to preach the gospel—not with wisdom and eloquence, lest the cross of Christ be emptied of its power" (1 Cor. 1:17 NIV).

So swap rescue stories, love stories, battle stories, and before-and-after stories. Our friends have them too.

Put it together.

Jesus keeps getting the glory and getting translated everywhere storytellers are bold to swap and step into more.

19 Practice Makes Permanent

Imagine a jar of a thousand beads. If you are learning the language of culture, then every time you practice paying attention to culture, you take out a bead. If you are learning the language of Christ, then every time you practice praying for someone, you take out a bead.

When the jar is empty, you have completed Translating Jesus 101. Fill the jar up again and work through level 201. I learned of this concept in Greg McKeown's book *Effortless*. His Spanish professor friend emphasizes that practice will most definitely include mistakes. These mistakes lead to accelerated learning. "The faster they make those mistakes, the faster they will progress. . . . There is no mastery without mistakes."[1]

McKeown says that many people don't practice because they don't want to mess up. As disciples we don't know all the answers we assume people will ask of us. We don't feel good enough or mature enough in our faith. We take the posture that to keep quiet is best. Not so, follower of Jesus. Not so.

Humans are programmed to practice in order to make perfect. I suggest we practice to make permanent. How is this? People retain both languages through attempts and mistakes as they practice over and over. Rather than "practice makes perfect"—a sugarcoated maneuver to get us to excel—how different to think "practice makes permanent." Perfection is not the goal but rather we strive to learn a skill and a language so it sticks and can be put into permanent practice.

You've read enough. It's time to take a bead out. Think through these three questions as you practice speaking Christ to culture and speaking to Christ about culture.

What moments do I find myself in? Your day is filled with many moments.

What languages do I practice? It matters who you are with to know if you are speaking culture or Christ.

What truths do I share? You have a message of hope to deliver. Give a word of truth to someone in the moment.

Let's look more in depth at how this gets lived out.

What moments do I find myself in?

Our moments happen in the marketplace, in Christian community, and in shared spaces. These are synonymous with the gate, the cross, and the table. Jesus is leading you to people who need His living hope. You are His translator. You know enough for any moment you find yourself in. I can promise this to you, because He who promised is faithful!

If every human is a unique creation of God, then every moment with every human is significant. What you say or don't say, what you do or don't do, what truth you confirm or neglect is crucial to the human heart.

Are you talking to parents at the park?

Are you leading a meeting?

Are you at a medical appointment?

Are you sitting by someone on the bus or plane?

Are you in the car with others?

Are you getting a haircut?

Are you in the classroom?

Are you eating at a restaurant?

Christ is at work everywhere. You are the temple of God, so you bring the presence of God wherever you go. If you only see Him in religious settings, you are missing out on 90 percent of His work. Maybe more.

Luke documents Jesus's time with two of His followers post-resurrection. They shared a moment as they walked and conversed about the recent events in Jerusalem. They had no idea the man with them was Jesus Himself. It wasn't until they were at the table and Jesus assumed the host role and broke the bread that their eyes were opened and they realized why their hearts were burning. This is happening with Christians today. We are representing Jesus in moments, and people don't even know He is in their midst. Christians can know because we see Him working or we believe by faith He is working in ways we can't see. Then we trust Him to open eyes and set hearts on fire.

The most opportune moments of your day are when you are in your sweet spot of your unique calling, because your God-given gifts and abilities are just naturally flowing. Teaching in a classroom or a small group. Leading a team or an organization.

Helping others heal or thrive. Working with your hands. Serving those in need. Learning to grow.

It's in these moments you are most alive and most yourself, so why not seize the chance to practice a language or two?

I took out a number of beads as I spent countless hours in the schoolyard with our kids over the years. Those beads represented ongoing conversations with other parents about beliefs, parenting, and fears. Beads also included a sad awareness of kids full of apathy and anger and empty of respect for others and themselves. I'm certain I looked sad on the playground sometimes, just like the two followers who were walking to Emmaus with Jesus but didn't know it. I knew Jesus. I couldn't find Him at school. I looked as though I had lost Him.

Can you identify with faith that feels high at church and depressingly low in culture? These followers could. Their faith was high a few days prior as they adored Jesus riding into Jerusalem. Now they thought Him dead and His body stolen.

"O foolish ones, and slow of heart to believe," Jesus said to them in Luke 24:25. Jesus needed these followers to invite Him into a moment. He was eagerly waiting to reveal Himself. I picture giddy Jesus. Today, He needs you and me to invite Him into moments too. We bring Him with us. We turn the key of hospitality with one another, and Jesus appears. It was at mealtime at the table that these two followers recognized Jesus. It will be in moments when both languages are spoken, when you are attentive to culture and prayerful in spirit, that Christ will make His presence known.

I want to live this post-resurrection life! I want to see Him appear, vanish, reappear, urge, speak, recline, break bread, and unlock. Dorothy Day left this challenge for followers:

We cannot love God, unless we love each other, and to love we just know each other. We know him in the breaking of bread, and we know each other in the breaking of bread, and we are not alone anymore.[2]

You have something to offer in every moment you are in. If you put this truth into practice, you will be translating Jesus on an ongoing basis.

Picture a moment you found yourself in today. What language was appropriate for you to practice?

What languages do I practice?

Culture or Christ or both? Following Jesus takes place at the gate, the cross, and the table. You'll encounter some of the same people at each place. You are learning. You are paying attention. You pray for others. You are asking questions. You bring up your faith, giving space for wonder.

If Abraham by faith can go without knowing where he was going, surely we can go into a moment and conversation by faith not knowing where it will go either (Heb. 11:8).

The Bethlehem shepherds showed up with nothing but a hunch. They didn't know what was waiting for them in the moment. These herders of sheep were made comfortable in the setting of a stable and conversed in the cultural moment and yet got to praise God together. Those present were bilingual, speaking culture and Christ.

We show up to give but also to receive. It's in translating Jesus that we ourselves experience more of His love and more of His presence, regardless of the spoken or unspoken language.

Practice this in your own home, with your own family, or with a close friend.

What moment am I in? I'm at home cooking dinner and the kids are doing homework. *What language do I practice?* Because everyone in my home now follows Jesus, I can pray with them and for them, listen about their days at the gate, and pay attention to what truth they need to hear or be reminded of. *What truth do I share with my kids?* "Jesus is honored by the way you chose what was right today." "I'm proud to be your mom." "Jesus was with you every moment today." "And let's not forget . . . it's trash night tonight!"

What moment are you in? Perhaps you're at a birthday dinner for a friend. Not everyone around the table is a follower of Jesus. In your heart, you can pray for God to give you love, place you strategically, help you listen, and guide conversation. You can ask simple questions. You can mention your faith if it's helpful to the moment. You can share truth no matter your skill set or expertise in their field. You can introduce hope that is found in Jesus if they mention pain or a problem. You can also just talk about how you know the guest of honor, and that's okay.

Jesus modeled how to use Scripture appropriately to enhance the moment. He determined who He was with and then used the Old Testament to show how the culture did life and would add what He brought to it. He challenged the curious to love one another, even their enemies. On many occasions, He said, "You've heard it said, but I say . . ." to show people what is important and right. He told the tired and worn out that He could give them rest. He blessed the poor, the sad, and the grieving. In connecting with culture and speaking about Himself, He was speaking both languages, therefore speaking to the admirer, the curious, and the follower.

Don't be afraid to ask, "Do you know Jesus?" My friend Hagar, affectionately known as Nana, was in the hospital on a ventilator and fighting breast cancer. I spent one morning with her, reading the Scriptures and praying for healing. Nana couldn't talk because of the tubes in her mouth. Her daughter could tell when she wanted to write something and would hand her a red pen and paper on a clipboard. When the doctor came in to check her stats, I needed to move to the other side of the bed, and as I did so, Nana gripped my hand. Simultaneously I felt a strong sense in my spirit to ask the doctor if she knew Jesus. So I asked her. It felt like I'd let the cat out of the bag. No turning back.

"I'm an atheist," the doctor replied.

Nana squeezed my hand again, and this time she didn't release the pressure.

"Nana is squeezing my hand, and I believe she wants you to know how much Jesus loves you," I said. Nana relaxed her grip.

"I respect my patients and what they choose to believe," the doctor said. She finished up her tasks and left—I sensed she was a little more flustered than she had been when she entered.

I looked at Nana. She squeezed my hand again. I prayed out loud with her for the doctor—for God to bring salvation to Nana's body and to the doctor's life.

That evening, I thought of the doctor again. I wondered if she was thinking about Jesus a little more. The Spirit was in the hospital room connecting me and Nana through our hands, and we were practicing both languages. The doctor's answers determined what Nana and I did next.

A week passed, and Nana was sitting up—then standing up. The doctor conceded that she didn't know the ways of our God and miracles could happen. Nana told the doctor, "Yes, my God is still in the miracle business!"

The question, "Do you know Jesus?" was not offensive. It profoundly touched a nerve, and that nerve sent an uncomfortable response to the doctor's brain. If Jesus Himself came and not everyone was receptive, you can assume not all will receive His love through you either. "But to all who did receive him, who believed in his name, he gave the right to become children of God" (John 1:12). This is why we keep translating Jesus. People are unpredictable. Who will receive? Who will one day understand? Can God really save that person?

When I ask you if you speak English, that's not wrong, and the answer determines the direction of our conversation. It makes it easier to converse. It affects the level at which we listen. If you don't speak English, or not very well, I'll have to increase my attention and watch your body language more closely.

If they do know Jesus, follow up by asking, "What's your relationship with Him like?"

Every bit of the human being belongs to God. You can't separate God from people. We are His design and His creation. For "in him we live and move and have our being" (Acts 17:28). We all relate to Him in some way. Asking "What's your relationship with Him like?" gives you time to listen, share your personal story, and create space for wonder.

Picture yourself practicing the necessary language. What truth needs to be shared to release Christ's love in the moment?

What truths do I share?

People can always use a kind, truthful word. Followers of the Way speak life. We offer encouragement.

As she greets you at the counter: "You have a beautiful smile."

As he serves you the artistic cappuccino: "You are really talented."

As you see the person routinely: "It's really good to see you today."

As you pass him walking the dog: "What a gorgeous day we have been given!"

As you leave the doctor: "You are great at taking care of so many people."

As you notice a service worker: "What you're doing is making a difference."

Determine the truth you share based on what people say or on their current actions or situation. What do they need?

You can ask, "Can I pray for you? What can I pray for you about?" People are very open to prayer. Most people believe there is a greater power in their time of need. Pray in the name of Jesus.

"I'm having trouble sleeping."

Jesus, the one You love is restless at night. Scripture says You can quiet her with Your love and will rejoice over her with singing. I invite You to orchestrate the most beautiful evening concert in her room tonight. May she know, undoubtedly, You are with her and You are rest. In Jesus's name.

"I'm depressed."

Jesus, the one You love is depressed. Show him how much You care for him in this very specific area of his life. Give him peace that passes all human understanding, and then may he share his testimony with another. In Jesus's name.

"My friend is in trouble or sick."

Jesus, the one You love cares for her friend. Also the other one You love is sick or in trouble. You care for the brokenhearted and have the power to heal. We call on You to make this person well so they see You are good and may live to tell this story. In Jesus's name.

"I've got some decisions to make."

Jesus, the one You love needs wisdom. He wants help to do what's good and right, and I pray You bless him with Your favor and wisdom. I pray he and others affected by Your gift of wisdom will acknowledge You are the gift giver and care so much for him. In Jesus's name.

We are to always have an answer, wrote Paul, even if the answer is along the lines of "I haven't experienced that, but I talk to someone daily who has" (see Col. 4:2–6). We know enough to have put our faith in Jesus and continue to follow Him daily. We have the message of hope, and we must share it with people who are desperate for it. Throughout this book, I've written a few ways to converse about our faith. For example, you can use this approach from chapter 7 as you share about Jesus being the way to salvation and freedom: Go narrow. Go through. Go wide.

And remember, the Good News can be given in three simple sentences:

1. Jesus loves you.

   "We love because he first loved us" (1 John 4:19).

2. Love Him back.

   "If you love me, you will keep my commandments" (John 14:15).

3. Love one another.

   "By this all people will know that you are my disciples, if you have love for one another" (John 13:35).

Nikole asked me at the café, "But what do I give Jesus for what He supposedly has given me?"

I said something like, "You love Him back. You turn from anything you've been following and follow Him. That's how you love Him back. It's the simplest, hardest reality on earth."

I believe this truth is for you. Jesus prays for those with whom you will share His Good News. This means He expects and trains His disciples to share Him. He prays for you and those who will follow Him because of you translating Him to others. Jesus said, "My prayer is not for them alone. I pray also for those who will believe in me through their message" (John 17:20 NIV). Let us love one another. Genuinely love one another. No gimmicks, sales pitches, time-shares, or gold stars are we pursuing.

Jesus has changed my life, and I care too much not to introduce you to Him.

Put it together.

Share what you know about God. Pray about what you don't know about life.

20 Read the Scriptures

Not everyone wants Jesus. But more do than we realize. We cannot predict what our love will do and who will receive it. We also cannot let this unpredictability keep us from explaining the hope we have in Him.

In the years that Jesus walked the earth, when He saw the crowds, the individuals, did He see who would trust Him and who would not? This would be far too great for a human to carry and comprehend—to see the future of all our friends and family and know their rejection, hurt, abandonment, and lack of faith in us. Yet Jesus still did what He came to do, regardless of my response to Him or my neighbor's response to Him. I once heard Steve Cuss, who has written on leadership anxiety, share how Jesus stood for truth, and if it offended someone He didn't run after that person to soften it or change it up.[1] This has everything to do with Christ's response to me and you. He doesn't waver because of our acceptance or rejection. Jesus still loves us all.

I don't understand how faith all works—me believing and not always certain of what I believe—but a mustard seed in me says it's true. God is real. Jesus's story pans out. What this size faith has allowed me to see is enough. I know it is true in the times when love won over the nastiness in my heart, when generosity welled up and spilled out, when a denial in our adoption process became overturned, when I told Charleston Jesus loves him, when hundreds in San Francisco have said yes to believing in Jesus. He is real and is very much found alive in relationship.

Living out your faith to those around you will be strange, awkward, weird, and misunderstood. Why wouldn't it be? You believe in an invisible God and have put your faith in Him for eternity's sake, and you work to live a disciplined life focused on Jesus's teachings. You really believe He created you, loves you so much He sent His Son Jesus to die for you and your sins and show you how to live this life on earth with Him, and sent His Spirit to dwell within you to make it possible.

Such a life will be attractive to others too. This will only happen because the Spirit of Christ is knocking on the door to their hearts, and they are curious, convicted, and conversational.

Living out your faith because it's personal and practical will cause you to experience great joy and great loss. Your faith in Jesus desires community with Christians, even as you suffer alongside one another in this life. The great loss comes as you watch people choose to make fun of God, reject Him, or put their faith in another.

Paul said his precious life had value as he got to translate Jesus (Acts 20:24). The New Testament is basically Jesus and Paul in community and culture. They were both on mission! Paul was one of the earliest translators of Jesus as the Good News started to spread. He is credited with taking this message to many gentile nations.

As Paul and other early translators of Christ loved one another, their very lives created space for wonder from the curious and admirers. Paul addressed the cultural idols of his day, and it's recorded at the close of the great book of Acts that his life was unhindered. As you become bilingual, you'll discover your life, too, gives space for wonder, addresses the elephants, and is unhindered.

Give space for wonder.

Read the Scriptures. At 3:00 p.m. on a weekday, two Christians who had the Spirit of the living God in them ministered to a lame man, and this act of love caused others to wonder about Jesus.

One day Peter and John were going up to the temple at the time of prayer—at three in the afternoon. Now a man who was lame from birth was being carried to the temple gate called Beautiful, where he was put every day to beg from those going into the temple courts. When he saw Peter and John about to enter, he asked them for money. Peter looked straight at him, as did John. Then Peter said, "Look at us!" So the man gave them his attention, expecting to get something from them.

Then Peter said, "Silver or gold I do not have, but what I do have I give you. In the name of Jesus Christ of Nazareth, walk." Taking him by the right hand, he helped him up, and instantly the man's feet and ankles became strong. He jumped to his feet and began to walk. Then he went with them into the temple courts, walking and jumping, and praising God. When all the people saw him walking and praising God, they recognized him as the same man who used to sit begging at the temple gate called Beautiful, and they were filled with wonder and amazement at what had happened to him. (Acts 3:1–10 NIV)

Peter and John were at the gate and translated Jesus to the man, and others got space to wonder. Remember that what happens at the gate doesn't stay at the gate! Peter and John had reclined at many tables with Jesus and picked up His confidence and certainty, and so they made eye contact with the man. Eye contact is becoming a lost practice, yet when used, it's a powerful connection. What courage and confidence they had to engage with this lame man and believe anything that happened was of God. So the man gave them his attention, and they gave him Jesus! Everyone knew him as a beggar at the gate. No one ever thought of him as someone who could come inside the temple.

Pastors preach all year long, yet they tend to be most expectant on Easter Sunday. A visitor making his annual pilgrimage to church one Easter was inspired enough to share the pastor's message with his family. This Easter message got watched again and again, causing some of the family to return to their faith and others to wonder. The father of the family wrote the pastor to say, "It was my son who came to your church." Create space for wonder.

A Christ follower looked for moments to share Jesus with her neighbor, yet none seemed appropriate. One day, the neighbor shared that her brother had died. The Christ follower listened and sympathized, and she committed to pray for her neighbor. Days later, they had dinner together. The neighbor commented on the Christ follower's joy and thanked her for the lovely sympathy card. How this Christ follower lived in front of her neighbor left space for wonder.

Peter and John said, "As for us, we cannot help speaking about what we have seen and heard" (4:20 NIV). Let the story speak for itself! Remember, Sundays are for swapping stories. Mondays through Saturdays are for stepping into stories. Peter and John went back to their own people and shared their story, and everyone praised God together. Our stories erupt with praise from even more people. Then, because of what happened with Peter and John, the rest of the people prayed they too would be able to speak with great boldness (v. 29).

Address the elephants.

Read the Scriptures. Paul addressed the elephant in the room. He addressed the idols in the culture. First-century Athens, Greece, was no different from where you live: people were chasing after other theories and things to satisfy. Paul was no different than you are. You also follow Jesus and believe better for others.

> While Paul was . . . in Athens, he was greatly distressed to see that the city was full of idols. So he reasoned in the synagogue with both Jews and God-fearing Greeks, as well as in the marketplace day by day with those who happened to be there. (17:16–17 NIV)

Paul, who at one time did everything against Jesus, now did everything for Jesus. He showed up in Athens and was greatly distressed by what everyone had made into their little gods. It didn't matter if he was at the marketplace or the synagogue; Paul tried to get the Athenians to see that Jesus was better. He told them they were creating their own religions where they were in control, putting their expectations on things and theories that couldn't hold the weight. When people haven't trusted in God, the very One who gives all people life and breath and everything else, they have another idol they worship.

Has your spirit ever been *provoked*? This is the term other translations use to describe what was happening to Paul as he moved around Athens. When I saw a religious theory social media account suggesting how to celebrate Easter as "exvangelicals," my spirit was provoked. When I heard a man shouting continually on a street corner that people were going to hell if they didn't repent, my spirit was provoked.

Do you notice that many people are living in fear? Fear is an idol. Do you notice that many people who get their candidate into office still seem dissatisfied? Politics is an idol. Paul noticed what people were worshiping, adoring, and fixated on. When people don't follow Jesus, they have infinite options for what or who they can put in that first-place position. "Anything goes" can go there. "What works for you" can take that place. So, what is it?

I want Jesus to be in that place, and I have to daily keep seeking Him first so that my everything else flows from that.

Paul preached the good news about Jesus and the resurrection, and folks debated him and didn't understand him. They needed a translation. This particular culture was up to date on all the latest news, as "all the Athenians and the foreigners who lived there would spend their time in nothing except telling or hearing something new" (v. 21). Yet the people of Athens said to Paul, "You bring some strange things to our ears. We wish to know therefore what these things mean" (v. 20). As we speak the language of Christ, we do so with mindfulness of culture. Many people have left Christianity because they didn't feel heard or seen by Christ followers. In Athens, Paul used their language, their poets, their statues, and their gods to explain Jesus. He was connecting and being bilingual. He told them in so many words, "I've walked around and have seen who you follow and to whom you give your allegiance." Some sneered at him, but others wanted to know more and some believed.

Later, in Jerusalem, Paul told his story in Hebrew (21:40–22:21). The people became more quiet and attentive because he spoke in their dialect and in ways they could identify. He recalled being present when Stephen was stoned. Paul had watched over the coats of the stone-throwers, happy with what was happening.

With Christ comes freedom for all who decide to follow His ways. Without Christ remains an alternative culture with far more limitations and ever-changing regulations. Nothing on earth is without restriction. Nothing culture can invite you into—no group, organization, or movement—is fully open. Asterisks are included. Limits and exclusions apply. I think this is what drives us to want to be our own person and build our own beliefs. The elephant in the room is the search for something that is vague with a sprinkle of value that sparks a bit of conviction without complicating one's life. Help others consider a search for Jesus instead. Suggest reading the account from either John or Luke.

Be unhindered.

Read the Scriptures. Paul was about twenty-seven years old at Stephen's stoning.[2] A few years later, Jesus turned his life around on the road to Damascus. Paul was about fifty-five years old when he wrote from Rome, and Luke said this about his season of life: "For two whole years Paul stayed there in his own rented house and welcomed all who came to see him. He proclaimed the kingdom of God and taught about the Lord Jesus Christ—with all boldness and without hindrance!" (28:30–31 NIV).

Followers of the Way will be working on translation for the rest of our lives. What Jesus is doing in our lives and how that can be a blessing to someone else is ongoing work.

From the Greek term we translate in verse 31 as "without hindrance," *akōlytōs,* I gather the following: Paul experienced all sorts of persecution and went to great lengths to let people know about the love of Jesus—unhindered.[3] He was completely open with his life. His confidence, as he said several times, was not in himself at all but in Jesus—unhindered. As you read the New Testament, much of which is Paul's letters, you see that no man could forbid him—unhindered.

The company of enthusiastic witnesses cannot be stopped! The movement that has been translating Jesus for two thousand years has been tried and tested. Either get caught up in it or choose to sit this one out. But if you are leaning toward sitting this one out because bringing the Good News of Jesus to others just isn't your thing, ask yourself this one important question: *If I plan to keep following Jesus, how must I live so that no one asks me about it?*

I look at the world, and Jesus keeps looking better and better. He's bigger than everything around me. He's more than everything around me. I can be in a conversation about someone else's pleasure-seeking weekend, accolades at a conference, or money-making mission, and believe I still have what this world will never afford and never be able to produce. I have Jesus. "If you love me, you'll keep my commands," Jesus told us (see John

14:15). Where do we find His commands? In the Bible. How do we love Jesus back? We keep His commands as we read the Bible.

C. S. Lewis asked, What is our culture doing with Christ? He wrote, "There is no question of what we can make of him, it is entirely a question of what he intends to make of us. You must accept or reject the story."[4] Following the Golden Rule (Matt. 7:12) or praying the Lord's Prayer (6:9–13) is not enough. Accepting or rejecting Jesus's teachings is not enough. Even the demons believe in Jesus (James 2:19). What's the difference, then? Christians choose Jesus.

Paul wrote to local contexts, local cultures. He wasn't writing to Americans. He was writing to the Romans, the Ephesians, and the Philippians. Paul studied Scripture. Paul studied culture. This is why he could communicate so well. He said, however, that "'knowledge' puffs up, but love builds up" (1 Cor. 8:1). He stood where people were before coming to Christ, to make the introductions so they might know, might believe, might choose. Paul really understood the freedom that is ours in Christ. He ministered to every culture he visited with this freedom that granted him confidence and authority.

> Though I am free and belong to no one, I have made myself a slave to everyone, to win as many as possible. To the Jews I became like a Jew, to win the Jews. To those under the law I became like one under the law . . . so as to win those under the law. To those not having the law I became like one not having the law . . . so as to win those not having the law. To the weak I became weak, to win the weak. I have become all things to all people so that by all possible means I might save some. I do all this for the sake of the gospel, that I may share in its blessings. (9:19–23 NIV)

How will you rewrite Paul's words to make them applicable for you? This passage from Paul can be severely taken out of context, but read it for yourself and ask the Holy Spirit to show you truth.

Here's my attempt:

> I love this freedom that is mine in Christ Jesus! While I want to see everyone I know come to put their trust in Jesus, their decision does not bind me, though I will do all I can to show them how much Jesus loves them. I am living like a San Franciscan, valuing our environment, science, and technological advancements. I try to treat the poor and the wealthy with the same dignity. I listen to all sorts of theories, fears, and worldviews in order that I may bring the hope of Jesus into conversations.

It didn't matter where Paul went; he took every possible opportunity to bring the language of love there. He did so by engaging culture and speaking his personal story. It's as if he were saying, "I was a Jew of Jews, a Hebrew of Hebrews; I knew the language. But I didn't come to you with lofty language but with the gospel" (see Phil. 3:5; 1 Cor. 2:1).

What is Jesus revealing to you?

My personal story of growing up in a Christian culture in the Bible Belt wasn't an automatic entry into the kingdom of God. Just because my dad was a pastor and my mom a missionary didn't guarantee my future. I had to learn Jesus was for me regardless of my upbringing. As I have lived in several different cultures in the United States, I have learned more about Jesus through each of them. He reveals Himself to me in truth.

Paul's words about "becoming all things" give me leave to take liberty in teaching us to become bilingual. Paul and all other followers of the Way can speak Christ and speak culture.

Put it together.

When you get to tell people about the love of Jesus, you are a part of the company of enthusiastic witnesses.

21 Connect with Christ and Culture

The most important thing followers of the Way can do while we're alive is to introduce people to Jesus. As a fellow disciple who continues to grow in translating Jesus, I believe we are all in a number of people's lives to make Christ's love known to them. Allow me to paraphrase E. Stanley Jones, a missionary to India: the Jesus of history must become the Christ of experience. We cannot just talk about Him—we must bring Him.[1] Evangelism is not just for a special class of Christians. It's what Jesus commissioned all of His disciples to do. As He was preparing to return to His Father in heaven, Jesus gave His initial disciples a brand-new command. It had everything to do with the reality of His physical self no longer being present and the disciples putting one crucial act into practice: love. They—and we—must love people like He has loved us, Jesus clearly stated. This is what will set us apart as Christians. Not *any* kind of love. The love of Jesus.

Throughout the writing of this book, I've often wondered, *If I could give a speech to my people after I'd truly paid attention to the language of my local culture, what would I say?* In this final chapter at the table, then, I've written three letters: a note to you who make up the company of enthusiastic witnesses, a note to my people, and a note to Jesus. We both have today; tomorrow is not guaranteed. Would you consider writing a letter of your own? What would you want your people to know?

A note to the company of enthusiastic witnesses.

If one can write urgently relaxed, this is the posture I take. I've prayed a thousand prayers for you and am just getting started. It energizes me to pray for you. My faith grows when I envision us going about our days full of the Spirit with heads held high in hope. One Christian after another is breathing out prayers every second of the day, creating a melody strung together that never stops and unleashing His Spirit and power on this earth in human hearts.

Holy Spirit, fill the witnesses reading this sentence with Your love and strength to go and share Jesus with others.

You are His light! Let the Father love you. Let the church be your home away from home. Let the world be your mission of love.

Following Jesus is learned in a lifetime, not at just one time in life. In fact, if you're living under the impression you've gotten all you need at a one-stop shop, you've been tricked. This is the richness and ease of inviting others to trust and obey Jesus—it's an unbalanced lifetime of learning and figuring it out and letting Him change you. The Christian life works best when you're Spirit-led. He will lead you into conversations and into pastures of rest. Jesus took time to get away to pray, and then He engaged in culture. Yearn for the Holy Spirit to lead you and love you. He will fill you with words at the gate and provide bounty at the table. This takes work on your part and isn't always neat and clean.

Christ established the church to be our home, refuge, sanctuary, and comfort and a safe, secure, nonjudgmental blessing to the city. The church ought to surprise the wanderer with grace because it is speaking both languages. This alone will overwhelm your people with His love. They will see how we love one another through Christ in a way that's not visible in their world without Christ. It ought to be obvious—a church swept up in His presence no matter the style but not minus the Spirit. Let us be caught up in His presence, for the church is God's home, and when we come together we form the body of Christ. This is the picture a divided world needs to see in a unified collection of Christ followers.

Jesus, keep us from living a segregated life apart from the world. Unite Your church in the call to seek shalom in all the places and people among whom You've sent us.

I asked three of my non-Christian friends this question: "If you did not know anything about Christianity, how would you want to be told about it?" Here are their responses:

- Tell me your story.
- Explain the facts.
- Invite me to what you're a part of.

Christ follower, this is how you translate Jesus to people who don't know Him. It was an atheist friend who told me that Christians think themselves too ignorant of Jesus to say anything when in truth whatever knowledge they have would greatly help her solidify or change her mind. You share what you know through your personal story. You explain the facts of the cross. You invite your non-Christian friends into meaningful conversations.

Translating Jesus needs to create awe of who He might be and how He could be in their lives. This is how I translate John 3:16: "God, our Father and Creator, loves the world, which definitely includes you and me. With intention and purpose, God sent His Son, Jesus, to die for our sins on the cross and then be resurrected. Anyone who will believe in Jesus and follow Him will have a forever relationship with Him and all the other believers in the kingdom of God." To quote the great translator, Paul, once again: "What we proclaim is not ourselves, but Jesus Christ as Lord" (2 Cor. 4:5). Be confident as you become bilingual.

We've got to make it personal so we can make it practical. Cover the inside of this book with names. Names of people who don't know just yet how much Jesus loves them. Will you decide to join me and the company of enthusiastic witnesses in translating Jesus with our very lives as we make this world a better place in Jesus's name?

A note to my people.

I've got your faces on my heart as I write, because this note is extremely personal. As I have studied our culture and learned from you, my friends and neighbors, I love you too much to let you tolerate anything and everything. I watch as it leads to tossing and turning in confusion and charging after the wind. I sense so much unhappiness in you. I have something better to offer. This is why I was sent to San Francisco and why I am still here. Jesus is a person you can know and with whom you can have a relationship. He is truth. Your search can end here, and you can spend your remaining life getting to know Him personally. He wants to talk with you and tell you things about your life.

He is more for the poor than this city will ever be.

He is full of justice and mercy.

He esteems women the most.

He advocates for our children, all of them.

He can make a way where there seems to be no way.

He can heal our people from their drug addictions.

He is able to restore what is broken.

He is stronger than any system.

If you're a feminist, you should want to know and love Jesus.

If you're depressed or lonely, you should want to talk with Jesus.

If you're frustrated with your identity or status, you should want to know what Jesus has to say.

I know Jesus. I talk to Him all the time about you. When I see broken windows and broken parts of our systems, I beg for His mercy. When I lose my patience with you, I pray He will forgive me and make me more loving like Him. When I see the wealth and the poverty, I pray for generosity and unity to take root. When I hear conversations that break Jesus's heart, I pray for truth to rule and reign. When the city grows dark with evil and lies, I pray for light to prevail. I do this out of love. Not because I have it all together; I've just found Jesus, and I'm seeking to orient my life around His teachings and life.

I'm a Christian and a hypocrite.

I'm a Christian and a worrier.

I'm a Christian and a control freak.

I'm a Christian and a spender.

I'm a Christian and can be apathetic, merciless, and unkind at times.

I'm a Christian who still struggles to forgive.

I'm a Christian who still has questions and doubts.

I'm a Christian and a work in progress to worry less, save more, forgive freely, trust Jesus, and keep asking questions.

This is my identity. It's an identity I've chosen yet also one given me. God chose me. Whether I identify with it or not doesn't change the fact that He is my Father and Creator. I can't undo that. He's your heavenly Father and Creator too. Not only do I accept this identity but I go a step further and identify as His follower, His child, and His creation.

What makes me a Christian is the decision I've made to give my life back to God, follow Jesus, and be led by the Holy Spirit. I choose to be a Christian. I choose to believe in Jesus Christ. I choose to follow His teachings with the help of His Spirit guiding me. He has changed my life and is changing my life. If I had purpose before, I really have purpose now. If I worried before, I worry less now. If I judged before, I have a check in my spirit now.

With Jesus in my life, I don't have to provide all the strength and muster up all the love to change myself and to love others. He is mighty and has overcome death; therefore, there is nothing He can't do in me. The Spirit is powerful, and wherever He is there is freedom. I'm more free as a Christian. Our culture paints a different picture.

I realize this world, particularly this nation, has many people who identify as Christian and don't practice the teachings of

Jesus, and they make it very confusing to anyone giving thought to the ways of Jesus. I can't fix that.

Wait, I can. I hope I live in such a way that you want to know this love Jesus has for you. I also love you. That's why I invite you to follow me as I follow Jesus. Not because I don't struggle—I just gave you some of the ways I do—but because Jesus is the only person to ever live who knows me and you inside and out, and defeated death so He could win us. Can you think of any reason not to love Jesus back by following Him? Jesus is far better than the kindest, most caring Christian you've ever known.

Have you ever come on anything quite like this extravagant generosity of God, this deep, deep wisdom? It's way over our heads. We'll never figure it out.

Is there anyone around who can explain God?
Anyone smart enough to tell him what to do?
Anyone who has done him such a huge favor
    that God has to ask his advice?

Everything comes from him;
Everything happens through him;
Everything ends up in him.
Always glory! Always praise!
    Yes. Yes. Yes. (Rom. 11:33–36 Message)

God is so good. I mean *so good*. He loves you so much. And with God, you don't have to throw away your desires. You get to give them to Him, and He does wonders with them! My dad loves sports. He majored in physical education in college, and then God called him to be a preacher. God didn't take his love for sports away. He's had a lifetime as a preacher to also referee, coach, go to some of the greatest games, play hundreds of rounds of golf, and be a chaplain for local high school teams. My pastor husband, Ben, wanted to major in business but was scared to give his speech in speech class so he dropped the class and changed his major to sociology. God has led Ben to start a church in an influential global city where he gets to lead hundreds of people who lead businesses and teams and give powerfully practical weekly sermons. I thought I'd be a missionary in another country. Following Jesus didn't lead me away from that but into *more*. He has me in a city to which He brings people from many nations, and I get to host them and befriend them.

You, my friend, are actually living out some of Jesus's teachings. You're giving to the poor, honoring your parents, praying to God on a case-by-case basis, caring for your enemies, overcoming evil with good, turning the other cheek at work, and doing for others who can't do for themselves. Have you considered following Him? It begins right here with a prayer.

When you pray to Jesus, you kick-start faith—believing in Someone outside of yourself. When you confess that you can't save yourself, there's good news because Jesus did so for you on the cross—that's the first step of faith in Him. Now you're in Jesus. Everything you do, you do in Him and He in you. Can you envision His power, grace, love, forgiveness, Word, and Spirit running through you? If this can't make for great rejoicing, what will?

Pray this prayer:

Jesus, I believe You love me. I make a decision to love You back by putting my life back in Your hands where it belongs. From this day forward, I choose to let people know I follow You by the way I love them.

A note to Jesus.

Jesus, I'm worn out and running to You at the same time. I've just poured my heart out to everyone I know and don't know. What I have left are my empty hands.

I pray for more of You. I pray for more of Your love. Come, Holy Spirit. I open my mind to You. I open my eyes to You. I open my nose, ears, and mouth to You. I give You my hands. Put in them what I need to obey You. Take out of my hands what will get in the way. I give You my body, my legs and feet; direct me and lead me where You want me to go. I can go down that dark hole and feel like I've got nothing to offer others and can be extremely inward focused. Come rescue me from a life of self-absorption and negativity. I repent and walk into truth and life that is only found in You.

Lead me to tables where I can dine with sinners and You.

Lead me to the cross daily, for I need to practice radical repentance.

Lead me into Your gates with praise.

No one loves me like You love me, Jesus. Where would I be without You? I'm so glad I don't have to wonder that anymore. You prayed with joy and a fullness of the Holy Spirit, and I ask for the same. I praise God, for You take pleasure in showing Your childlike faith-followers hidden things. You and Your Father enjoy intimacy and offer this gift to me as well. It is the sweetest, deepest, richest potential of a relationship I can ever have. To know You intimately, I just can't explain it. Please tell me and reveal to me these hidden things, for I come as Your child, I come as Your child. I'm listening. You've given me friends who don't know You yet, and again, I ask that You will open their hearts and minds to Your love. I realize they are far more valuable to You than to me, but You have given us all a choice, and I pray You direct their steps to choose You.

I can't believe You love me like You do. I pray I never lose the wonder of You. I also pray I never lose this love for my city, my people. I ask You to send more disciples to be our friends and to grow Your church here.

Jesus, I want my faith in action to amaze You. It did for the four followers who brought their paralyzed friend to you. You saw *their* faith and told their friend that his sins were forgiven. The faith in the faith-filled healed the body and soul of an unbeliever. This went beyond the five of them. This continues to be Your plan. You called the first disciples and made them translators. On their own, they could not fulfill their purpose. Only You could. They made a decision to obey You. Then You rewarded them. They worshiped You. Others joined in. You commissioned them: what You did for them, they would go and do for You out in the world. How can my faith in You set my people free? I'll do whatever it takes to bring them to You.

Put it together.

Even if this world gives up on us or Jesus, we must not give up on this world. His love is the only way.

"How Do You Even Become a Christian?"

If someone were to ask you, "How do you even become a Christian?" what would you say? Always share your story—your life before Jesus, meeting Jesus, and your life presently. But sometimes people want a how-to guide. Sometimes, people need H.E.L.P.

Hear and decide.
When you consider what you've heard about Jesus, do you want to follow Him?

What else do you need to hear about Jesus to follow Him?

Exercise trust.
Say to Jesus that you believe He is who He claims to be, and put your faith in Him.

Live for Him.
Make regular choices to read the Bible, connect with Him in prayer, and spend time in Christian community.

Pass along the news.
Jesus is good news, and the best thing you can do for others is tell them about Him!

Acknowledgments

The writer at the desk is indeed writing in isolation, but (for me, at least) this isolation must be surrounded by community, be it the community of faith, village, church, city.

Madeleine L'Engle, *Walking on Water: Reflections on Faith and Art*

Hopefully your soul is full but you have saved room for dessert, because this is the sweetest moment of the book. This book has ended up in a place so different from where it started. It has a different name, insides, and audience. The book's heartbeat began in November 2019 after I had a Tolkien encounter and a Holy Spirit infusion about the remnant of God's people. Then we entered a worldwide pandemic and that remnant became more clearly defined for me: those who hold to their faith in Jesus despite the pull to what is popular and political. As November 2020 slowly arrived, I wondered if my initial thoughts were changing form. Was my message to encourage the church to keep going, or was it to figure out how to share the same Good News in a new way?

It has been the community of faith, village, church, and city who have surrounded me on this journey up to these final pages.

The **village** is on the outskirts of town. Through conversations, Carey Nieuwhof, Mark Batterson, and Emily Freeman responded to my initial dreams with clarity and wise counsel. Emily has said before, "Your ideal reader is not determined by who ends up reading your work. Your ideal reader is determined by who you have in mind when you write your work." My steadfast editor Andrea Doering knows me and pulls out of me what I don't even know is there. Andrea helped me identify my two readers: my friend who has just started following Jesus and is still attracted to the ways of this world, and my other friend who has been a Christian for decades and abstains from the world. Many other people at Revell had their gifted hands on this book, and I'm so glad. I'm also thankful for the folks at the Fedd Agency: Esther for her intensely gifted literary vision, Kyle for naming the book, Danielle for managing the team efforts, and Alli for styling the proposal. Ariel Curry coached me and gave me space to process out loud when I came upon obstacles in my head. Hope*Writers is a true village of cheerleaders for every writer, and I'm glad I live among them. The town of Yountville loaned me and Ben their sidewalks and irresistible roses on a weekly basis to take a break from work. I cannot even list all the musicians and songwriters who lifted me to the heavenlies to imagine all that is possible through the written word.

The **faith-filled** live all over the world. To the ones who have no idea their faith fueled mine, thank you. Dallas Jenkins created *The Chosen* television series and helped Jesus become more real to me, and he's teaching me how to get used to *different*. Pete Greig prayed for a mom in the audience at the Alpha conference in 2022 who had a strong love for her family and her church and her city, and that prayer boosted my confidence as I finished up the manuscript. My writer friend Rachel Dodge consistently sharpens what I give my readers. Chris Grigg prayed early morning prayers, and her 6:00 a.m. texts got me to the writing desk. Candace Collette set aside her tasks and took drafts on her travels, all to give me constructive feedback in the immediate; she also covered me and you in prayer. Elizabeth Moore has kept me young and fresh in my writing and faith as we flesh both out in our beloved cities. Alpha friends worldwide have reminded me how real Jesus is and how inviting is His kingdom.

It has always been the **church**, the followers of Jesus, who refuse to let me live or write in isolation. Jess Condrey, Bea Moraza, Rachael Wade, Ben Lee, and others were determined to be my companions with this book. I'm grateful for my pastors, Ben Pilgreen, Lindsey Lee, Will Moraza, and Seth Condrey, and for our leadership team at Epic Church who lead me in worship, Word, and wisdom every week. Jonathan Mayes and Mike and Betsy Montague took keen interest in my soul as I wrote.

I've had countless disciples I've learned from with this book, and I want you to know who they are. Alister McGrath's and John Stott's works inspire me. John Wimber's and Sandy Millar's obedience to Jesus continues to have a ripple effect. Dane Ortlund, David Benner, and Dr. Robert E. Coleman, I hope my writing draws people to Jesus like yours has done for me. Madeleine L'Engle and Dorothy Sayers are magical women who mysteriously echo that my voice matters. Eugene Peterson still pastors me through his books. Nicky and Pippa Gumbel, I make no apology for the tears that once stained this page. Your love for His people is contagious, and I'm just one human infected. J. R. R. Tolkien was kind to sit by me on a plane back in November 2019.

He pointed me to the remnant, and the Spirit opened my eyes to the moment—a moment I didn't see coming.

My **city** has been written off by many Christians and even culture as God-forsaken, but Jesus is alive and dwells in San Francisco. I see Him here every day. I'm grateful for every disciple and church in our forty-nine square miles who are becoming bilingual. Once again, I write a book filled with stories from my city because Jesus is being translated and received here! Many offered their stories graciously because they want their lives to point people to Jesus—too numerous to name here, but they fill this book. Thank you. I've said it to you privately, but here it is in published print. May your lives and stories keep leading others to the love of Jesus, and may our city experience revival.

My **family** means everything to me. God in His kindness gave me four incredible kids, not just for me to raise but for them to raise me. Elijah, Sam, Kavita, and Asher have lavished ridiculous amounts of grace on me and continue to teach me how to share Jesus. My husband, Ben, has prayed over me daily and then proceeded to hand me the pen and paper to get about my calling to write this book.

I close by acknowledging **Jesus**. You're the One who has my whole heart. You reign. You are the reason I write. You've been most present, most patient. It's always been You. When words were invisible, not coming, and clogged, You gave me the shovel to dig and find them. You sat by me when I wrote. Your Spirit was in me, and I cried as I wrote because I know and I absolutely felt You giving me the words—electronically, collaboratively, worshipfully. Jesus, I love You so much.

Notes

Introduction

1. Alister McGrath, *Mere Discipleship: Growing in Wisdom and Hope* (Grand Rapids: Baker Books, 2019), 107.
2. McGrath, *Mere Discipleship*, 106.
3. Ludwig Wittgenstein, *Tractatus Logico-Philosophicus*, 471st ed. (Mineola, NY: Dover, 1998), 89.

Chapter 1 Learn the Language

1. John Stott, *Basic Christianity*, 3rd ed. (Grand Rapids: Eerdmans, 2017), 112.
2. New World Encyclopedia, s.v. "Johannes Kepler," accessed October 20, 2022, www.newworldencyclopedia.org/entry/Johannes_Kepler.
3. John Stott, *The Contemporary Christian: Applying God's Word to Today's World* (Downers Grove, IL: InterVarsity, 1992), 13.

Chapter 3 Meet the People

1. Michael Ramsey, *Image Old and New* (London: SPCK, 1963), 14.

Chapter 4 Listen to Stories

1. Ralph G. Nichols and Leonard A. Stevens, "Listening to People," *Harvard Business Review*, September 1957, https://hbr.org/1957/09/listening-to-people.
2. Stott, *Contemporary Christian*, 222.
3. Barna, "What Makes an Engaging Witness, as Defined by Gen Z," Barna, November 10, 2021, https://www.barna.com/research/gen-z-witness/.
4. Nichols and Stevens, "Listening to People."
5. Winn Collier, *A Burning in My Bones: The Authorized Biography of Eugene H. Peterson, Translator of The Message* (Colorado Springs: Waterbrook, 2021), 239.

6. Gary Keller with Jay Papasan, *The One Thing: The Surprisingly Simple Truth Behind Extraordinary Results* (Portland, OR: Rellek Publishing Partners/Bard Press, 2012), 104.

Chapter 5 Practice the Language

1. Collier, *Burning in My Bones*, 129.
2. Rich Villodas, *The Deeply Formed Life: Five Transformative Values to Root Us in the Way of Jesus* (Colorado Springs: Waterbrook, 2021), 194.

Chapter 6 Read the Scriptures

1. "Ethiopia People 2020," Countries of the World, accessed October 27, 2022, https://theodora.com/wfbcurrent/ethiopia/ethiopia_people.html.
2. Kenneth Scott Latourette, *A History of Christianity*, vol. 1 (New York: Harper and Brothers Publishers, 1937), 59.
3. Josh McDowell, *More Than a Carpenter* (Carol Stream, IL: Tyndale, 2009), 66, 69.

Chapter 7 Connect with Christ and Culture

1. Joseph Loconte, *A Hobbit, a Wardrobe, and a Great War: How J. R. R. Tolkien and C. S. Lewis Rediscovered Faith, Friendship, and Heroism in the Cataclysm of 1914–1918* (Nashville: Nelson, 2017), 152.
2. Stott, *Basic Christianity*, 125.
3. Karl Rahner, "The Divine Dawning," in *Watch for the Light: Readings for Advent and Christmas* (Walden, NY: Plough Publishing, 2014), 74, emphasis in original.
4. If you've read *Love Where You Live*, you'll remember their names on the walls.

Chapter 8 Learn the Language

1. "The Water Cycle," Water Education Foundation, accessed October 27, 2022, https://www.watereducation.org/general-information/water-cycle.
2. Stott, *Basic Christianity*, 148–49.
3. McGrath, *Mere Discipleship*, 114.
4. "A Brief History of the Prayer, 'Come, Holy Spirit,'" Vineyard USA, accessed October 24, 2022, https://vineyardusa.org/library/a-brief-history-of-the-prayer-come-holy-spirit/.
5. John Wimber and Kevin Springer, *Power Evangelism*, rev. and updated ed. (Grand Rapids: Chosen, 2009), 56–57.

Chapter 9 Know the Landscape

1. See 2 Cor. 5:17; 1 Cor. 2:16; 2 Cor. 10:5.
2. Nicky and Pippa Gumbel, "Day 26, Why Does God Allow Suffering?," *Bible in One Year 2020 with Nicky Gumbel*, YouVersion Bible Plan, https://www.bible.com/reading-plans/17704-bible-in-one-year-2020-with-nicky-gumbel.
3. Oswald Chambers, *My Utmost for His Highest*, classic ed. (Grand Rapids: Discovery House, 2007), December 9.

4. As quoted in *Bread and Wine: Readings for Lent and Easter* (Walden, NY: Plough Publishing, 2003), 36.

Chapter 10 Meet the People

1. Dietrich Bonhoeffer, "Lectures to the Congregation in Barcelona," in *God Is on the Cross: Reflections on Lent and Easter* (Philadelphia: Westminster John Knox, 2012), 69.
2. Søren Kierkegaard, "Followers Not Admirers," in *Provocations: Spiritual Writings of Kierkegaard*, compiled and edited by Charles E. Moore (Walden, NY: Plough Publishing, 1999), 86.
3. As quoted in McDowell, *More Than a Carpenter*, 27.
4. Kierkegaard "Followers Not Admirers," in *Provocations*, 86.
5. Thomas à Kempis, "The Royal Road," in *Bread and Wine*, 36–37.

Chapter 11 Step into Stories

1. Dietrich Bonhoeffer, "The Coming of Jesus Christ in Our Midst," in *A Testament to Freedom: The Essential Writings of Dietrich Bonhoeffer*, edited by Geoffrey B. Kelly and F. Burton Nelson (San Francisco: HarperSanFrancisco, 1995), 186.

Chapter 12 Practice the Language

1. Sarah Bradford, *Harriet Tubman: The Moses of Her People* (Mineola, NY: Dover Publications, 2004), 44.
2. Bradford, *Harriet Tubman*, 44.
3. The Alpha Course, "Week 5: Why and How Do I Pray?," https://alphausa .org/.
4. Stott, *Basic Christianity*, 144.
5. Bonhoeffer, *God Is on the Cross*, 6.
6. Christoph Friedrich Blumhardt, "Action in Waiting," in *Watch for the Light: Readings for Advent and Christmas* (Walden, NY: Plough Publishing, 2001), 10.

Chapter 13 Read the Scriptures

1. Jason Murdock, "Humans Have More Than 6,000 Thoughts per Day, Psychologists Discover," *Newsweek*, July 15, 2020, https://www.newsweek.com/humans -6000-thoughts-every-day-1517963.
2. Adapted from Andy Stanley, "Investigating Jesus," sermon series, Northpoint Church, March 2022, https://northpoint.org/messages/investigating-jesus /somebody-had-to-tell.
3. Edith Stein, "Thy Will Be Done," in *Bread and Wine*, 168.
4. "Frequency of Reading the Bible among Adults in the United States from 2018 to 2021," Statista, accessed October 25, 2022, https://www.statista.com/statistics /299433/bible-readership-in-the-usa/; "In U.S., Decline of Christianity Continues at Rapid Pace," Pew Research Center, October 17, 2019, https://www.pewresearch .org/religion/2019/10/17/in-u-s-decline-of-christianity-continues-at-rapid-pace/.
5. I met Pastor Samuel Lamb in May 1996. This video tells more of his story: "Rev Samuel Lamb China and the Church in China," YouTube video, 23:46, uploaded by Rev Samuel Lamb China, January 26, 2015, https://youtu.be/ok 0KP8WD1Wg.

Chapter 14 Connect with Christ and Culture

1. New World Encyclopedia, s.v. "Johannes Kepler."

2. Martin Copenhaver, *Jesus Is the Question: The 307 Questions Jesus Asked and the 3 He Answered* (Nashville: Abingdon, 2014), 87.

3. I share this question from Christ follower Glenn Packiam, whom I heard at Alpha Conference, January 2022, Phoenix, Arizona.

4. "Strong's G2097: *euangelizō*," Blue Letter Bible, accessed December 5, 2022, https://www.blueletterbible.org/lexicon/g2097/kjv/tr/0-1/.

5. Robin Cornetet, "'Share Jesus without Fear' Author Honored for Evangelism Legacy," *Kentucky Today*, May 30, 2020, https://www.kentuckytoday.com/baptist-life/share-jesus-without-fear-author-honored-for-evangelism-legacy/article_b9665826-0db7-5497-a142-9e5dbf9c9fea.html.

Chapter 15 Become Bilingual

1. George MacDonald, *The Complete Fairy Tales* (New York: Penguin Books, 1999), 9.

2. Dorothy Day, "The Mystery of the Poor," in *Bread and Wine*, 316.

3. Eberhard Arnold, "Spirit of Fire," in *Bread and Wine*, 399.

4. Nellie Bowles, "How San Francisco Became a Failed City," *Atlantic*, June 8, 2022, https://www.theatlantic.com/ideas/archive/2022/06/how-san-francisco-became-failed-city/661199/.

5. When the Romans defeated the Greeks in 146 BC, they adopted the Greek style of reclining dining. "Jesus Reclined to Dine," Early Church History, accessed October 27, 2022, https://earlychurchhistory.org/food/jesus-reclined-to-dine/.

6. Ben Pilgreen, message at Epic Church, San Francisco, October 24, 2021.

7. Mark Sayers, *A Non-Anxious Presence: How a Changing and Complex World Will Create a Remnant of Renewed Christian Leaders* (Chicago: Moody, 2022).

8. S. Sudhar Singh, "I Have Decided to Follow Jesus," Timeless Truths, accessed December 5, 2022, https://library.timelesstruths.org/music/I_Have_Decided_to_Follow_Jesus.

Chapter 16 Know the Landscape

1. McGrath, *Mere Discipleship*, 44.

2. "Nones" are people who classify themselves as having no religious affiliation.

3. McGrath, *Mere Discipleship*, 109.

4. Michelle Boorstein, "Peloton Makes Toning Your Glutes Feel Spiritual. But Should Jesus Be Part of the Experience?," *Washington Post*, February 8, 2021, https://www.washingtonpost.com/road-to-recovery/2021/02/05/peloton-ally-love-robin-christianity-covid/.

5. Stott, *Basic Christianity*, 145.

6. Eugene Peterson's paraphrase of the parable has Jesus say it like this: "I want my house full!" (Luke 14:23 Message).

Chapter 17 Live with Your People

1. Bradford, *Harriet Tubman*, 28.

2. Leonardo Boff, *Jesus Christ Liberator: A Critical Christology for Our Time* (Maryknoll, NY: Orbis Books, 1978), 178.

3. Stott, *Basic Christianity*, 129.

4. Lorine McGinnis Schulze, "How Many Ancestors Do We Have?," Legacy News, August 4, 2016, https://news.legacyfamilytree.com/legacy_news/2016/08 /how-many-ancestors-do-we-have.html.

Chapter 18 Swap Stories

1. "Strong's H7307: *rûaḥ*," Blue Letter Bible, accessed December 5, 2022, https://www.blueletterbible.org/lexicon/h7307/kjv/wlc/0-1/.

2. Bradford, *Harriet Tubman*, 70.

Chapter 19 Practice Makes Permanent

1. Greg McKeown, *Effortless: Make It Easier to Do What Matters Most* (New York: Currency, 2021), 128.

2. Dorothy Day, *The Reckless Way of Love: Notes on Following Jesus* (Walden, NY: Plough Publishing, 2017), 120.

Chapter 20 Read the Scriptures

1. I heard Steve Cuss share this in a conversation with John Ortberg in "Overcoming the Five Idols: John Ortberg & Steve Cuss," YouTube video, 11:10, uploaded March 11, 2022, by Become, https://youtu.be/Dki3T0GP1WA.

2. "Timeline of the Apostle Paul," Blue Letter Bible, accessed October 27, 2022, https://www.blueletterbible.org/study/paul/timeline.cfm.

3. "Strong's G209: *akōlytōs*," Blue Letter Bible, accessed December 5, 2022, https://www.blueletterbible.org/lexicon/g209/esv/mgnt/0-1/.

4. C. S. Lewis, *God in the Dock: Essays on Theology and Ethics* (Grand Rapids: Eerdmans, 2014), 170.

Chapter 21 Connect with Christ and Culture

1. E. Stanley Jones, "The Christ of Experience," from *The Christ of the Indian Road* (Nashville: Abingdon, 1953).

Shauna Pilgreen, along with her husband, Ben, coleads Epic Church, a multiethnic congregation in the heart of San Francisco. She serves on the teaching team at Epic and as a network director for Alpha USA. She writes for "everyday evangelists" on her blog. Learn more at www.shaunapilgreen.com.

Connect with the Author at
www.ShaunaPilgreen.com

READ MORE FROM SHAUNA PILGREEN

love where you live

HOW *to* LIVE SENT *in* *the* PLACE YOU CALL HOME

shauna pilgreen

FOREWORD BY RANDY FRAZEE

With enthusiasm and contagious joy, Shauna Pilgreen gives readers the skills and guidance they need to reach out into their communities and spread God's redeeming love.

Revell

a division of Baker Publishing Group
www.RevellBooks.com

Available wherever books and ebooks are sold.

Be the First to Hear about New Books from Revell!

Sign up for announcements about new and upcoming titles at

RevellBooks.com/SignUp

@RevellBooks

Don't miss out on our great reads!

Revell

a division of Baker Publishing Group
www.RevellBooks.com